NORTHERN ARIZONA UNIVERSITY

NORTHERN ARIZONA UNIVERSITY

Buildings as History

∿

LEE C. DRICKAMER
AND PETER J. RUNGE

FOREWORD BY JOHN D. HAEGER
WITH SPECIAL CONTRIBUTIONS BY
THOMAS PARADIS AND BARBARA VALVO

THE UNIVERSITY OF ARIZONA PRESS
TUCSON

The University of Arizona Press
© 2011 The Arizona Board of Regents

www.uapress.arizona.edu

Library of Congress Cataloging-in-Publication Data
Drickamer, Lee C.
    Northern Arizona University : buildings as history / Lee C.
Drickamer and Peter J. Runge ; foreword by John D. Haeger and
with special contributions by Thomas Paradis and Barbara Valvo.
        p. cm.
    Includes bibliographical references and index.
    ISBN 978-0-8165-2981-0 (cloth : alk. paper)
    1. Northern Arizona University—Buildings—Guidebooks.
2. Architecture—Arizona—Flagstaff—Guidebooks. I. Runge,
Peter J., 1964– II. Paradis, Thomas W. (Thomas Wayne), 1970–
III. Valvo, Barbara. IV. Title.
    LD4011.N268D75 2011
    378.791'33—dc22
                                                    2010040824

Publication of this book was made possible in part by funding
from the Northern Arizona University Foundation.

Manufactured in South Korea.

16   15   14   13   12   11   6   5   4   3   2   1

We dedicate this book to everyone, past, present, and future, as members of the wonderful community that is Northern Arizona University. A special dedication to Melvin Hutchinson, whose extensive research and wonderful insights into the history of Northern Arizona University led to other histories of the institution and this book on the history of the buildings on campus.

CONTENTS

ILLUSTRATIONS

Figures

Maps and Aerial Photographs

FOREWORD

The heart of a university is the dynamic interaction of its students, faculty, and staff. The players in these roles change over time, providing a continuous flow of ideas, curriculum changes, teaching practices, athletics, performances, and personalities. Scholarly activities move forward with new ideas, inventions, and societal needs. The organization of academic units in a college like Northern Arizona University undergoes alterations over time, for curricular, financial, and historical reasons.

The history of higher education in America underwent a major shift in the years after World War II. Prior to the war, there were many schools, including Arizona State College at Flagstaff, whose major mission was preparing teachers for primary and secondary schools. After the war, many of these institutions moved toward a broader mission that included bachelor's and master's degrees in fields other than education. This happened at the Flagstaff institution, culminating in university status in 1966.

While the people who are the institution and the mission change over time, the buildings that comprise the campus remain for many years. In the case of Northern Arizona University, some of its buildings have witnessed more than one hundred years of educational history. The book you have in hand is a tale of the buildings that are the physical plant for the learning and scholarship of many generations. Buildings do indeed tell us a great deal about the history of education and about our university in particular.

Many of the changes on the Northern Arizona University campus mirror the changes in its mission. Before 1946, the campus consisted of little more than a dozen buildings of the historic North Campus. Over the ensuing three decades, expansion of the curriculum and significant increases in the student population, faculty, and staff were accompanied by a continual move southward, encompassing today's Central Campus and the new South Academic Center. At the end of the twentieth and beginning of the twenty-first centuries more buildings were added, most in locations within the existing campus and many with more specialized functions than was customarily the case in previous decades. More than eighty buildings have been added in the last fifty years, resulting in the current campus.

Anyone visiting the campus today will immediately realize that we are in the midst of a significant expansion of our physical plant. The needs of our society and the education of a new generation of students drive a need for new residence halls, research buildings, and facilities for health, recreation, and athletics. The master plan for the campus includes a gradual removal of traffic from interior spaces. New traffic patterns and parking facilities, some of which are already in place, will result in a central campus that is pedestrian and bicycle friendly with many green spaces.

I am very pleased to share with you a visual history of Northern Arizona University, as seen from the perspective of its physical plant. The book provides a fine presentation of photographs from the past and present, short text passages about each building, and a photo and biography for each of our buildings named for an important individual in the history of the campus. The collection will provide many memories for alumni, complement Flagstaff historical literature, and be a valuable resource for future generations.

John D. Haeger, President
Northern Arizona University
September 2009

This book is a joint effort. One of us (Lee Drickamer) is a biologist with a long-standing fascination with history, which began with a high school history teacher nearly fifty years ago. He has focused on both nineteenth-century American history and local history. He was on the board and served a term as president of the Berkshire County Historical Society in western Massachusetts. He has edited or authored four history books, including a postal history of Berkshire County, Massachusetts, and a volume of letters by and newspaper dispatches about a Civil War soldier who served in the 34th Massachusetts Volunteer Infantry.

The second author, Peter Runge, is the curator of manuscripts and digital content for the Cline Library Special Collections and Archives at Northern Arizona University. He has held that position since 2005. He obtained his education from Villanova University (BA), West Chester University (MA), and the University at Albany–State University of New York (MLS). Previously he worked in the special collections and archives libraries at the University of California–San Diego, Union College, and the University at Albany. This is his first book-length publication.

A common interest in the local history of Flagstaff and northern Arizona, and particular interest in the campus at Northern Arizona University, resulted in the present collaboration. Several individuals have written the history of Flagstaff, most notably Platt Cline (1976, 1994), Tom

Paradis (2003), and George Tinker (1969). The history of Northern Arizona University has been covered in depth by several authors (Cline 1983, 1990, 1999; Hutchinson 1972; Walkup 1984a,b), providing insights into the workings of this exceptional institution. While previous histories provide a record of the principal players, important events, and the tenor of the times, it became clear that there was no unified history of the physical structures comprising the campus. This book attempts to capture the physical development of Northern Arizona University.

Research on the project began in late summer 2006. With the assistance of countless members of the university and Flagstaff communities, we began collecting information, anecdotes, and photographs. This type of research is like being a detective, tracking leads to find particular bits of information, photographs, and details about buildings and people. Then there are the glorious moments when a wonderful staff person in the Special Collections and Archives finds another folder containing pictures not previously seen or a long-sought bit of information.

We have thoroughly enjoyed this endeavor. We hope that what you see gives you a sense of the history of the campus from the perspective of the physical structures that have served us for more than a century. Northern Arizona University alumni will, no doubt, have happy memories of many of the buildings and scenes depicted in this book.

ACKNOWLEDGMENTS

A project of this size and complexity requires a great deal of cooperation and assistance from many sources. Five people in particular aided our efforts immeasurably. Thomas Paradis, a faculty member in the Department of Geography and Public Planning at Northern Arizona University, is an expert on architectural styles. Together we walked the campus on a number of cold mornings in the winter of 2006–2007, taking notes and discussing the styles and features of every building from Old Main on the north end to the married student housing at the south end of campus. Tom shared his knowledge and we received an education in architecture. In addition to his essay "Interpreting the Northern Arizona University Landscape" in the front matter, he provided excellent input for the sections of each building description detailing architectural styles and elements and contributed the section on architecture that appears in the essay "Building Northern Arizona University" in the back matter.

Barbara (Bee) Valvo, former curator of visual materials at the Cline Library Special Collections and Archives at Northern Arizona University, tirelessly located many of the photographs showing the older structures on campus and dug into the archives for some elusive and rarely seen views deemed important for the book. We would also like to acknowledge the expertise and many hours that Jess Vogelsang, digital production supervisor at the Cline Library Special Collections and Archives, provided in the preparation of the historical images for publication.

Candace Awbrey, Mark Flynn, and their able assistants at Capital Assets and Services at Northern Arizona University compiled information on many of the campus buildings, providing detailed information for each structure.

Two people from the Bilby Research Center at Northern Arizona University were very instrumental in the later stages of the project. Victor Leshyk did a wonderful job with the maps. Eve Paludan used her editorial skills and amazing capacity to locate elusive bits of information to help put the finishing touches on the book. To each of these fine individuals we owe a special debt of gratitude. In addition, Drickamer is pleased to acknowledge the partial release from other duties during a sabbatical in spring 2008; this resulted in blocks of time to compile information, locate photographs, and write.

The late Melvin Hutchinson, whose book *The Making of Northern Arizona University* provides the basis for many other histories of the university, was a master at his craft. Without his efforts, we would not have the wealth of information needed to compile a volume such as this.

We thank the wonderful people at the University of Arizona Press, who handled myriad aspects of the production. In particular, we wish to express our appreciation to Dr. Allyson Carter, whose enthusiasm and support were critical to the project. Our work was edited and polished by Debra Makay; her "behind-the-scenes" efforts are sincerely appreciated. In addition, at the University of Arizona Press, we thank our production editor, Nancy Arora, for her advice and great work, and Scott De Herrera, who assisted Allyson on many occasions. At Northern Arizona University, Dan Boone was an important resource on various aspects of book preparation and production—we are most grateful for his advice and assistance. A hearty thanks to the various reviewers who aided our efforts, working with the manuscript and the University of Arizona Press.

As with any time-consuming endeavor of this nature, other duties or obligations were postponed to concentrate on the tasks associated with the book (all of which were fun and exciting). We acknowledge and thank departmental colleagues, students, and others at Northern Arizona University for putting up with the absences that allowed us to research and write. Drickamer is indebted to his wonderful wife, Judith Sellers, of the Northern Arizona University School of Nursing, for her advice, wise counsel, and enthusiasm over the several years needed to generate the book. Runge thanks colleagues at the Cline Library Special Collections and Archives for their assistance and dedication to the project, Lee Drickamer for his enthusiasm and invitation to work on this wonderful project, and his family, Vanessa and Malia, for their support and patience.

A host of other wonderful colleagues and friends acquired during our work gave us their time, knowledge, and advice. To each of them we express our sincere thanks. We hope you all enjoy the book—you helped to make it happen. The alphabetical list that follows is an attempt to thank all of these individuals; our apologies to anyone that we may have missed: Lee Altonna, Charles Avery, Russell Balda, Tom Bauer, Ramon Bazurto, Ryan Belnap, Sam Borozan, David Brumbaugh, Jason Bullard, Robert Crozier, Paul Davila, Tony DeLuz, T. C. Eberly, Richard Fernandez, Alan Flitcraft, William Griffen, Wolf (George IV) Gumerman, Ron Gunderson, Leo (Red) Haberlack, Lisa Heidinger, Angela Helmer, Bruce Hooper, Eugene Hughes, Harlan Johnson, Sandra Kowalski, Jerry Ladhoff, Evelyn Lewis, Barry Lutz, Michael Malone, Alyssa Manglesdorf, Linn Montgomery, Jane Mulrooney, Lisa Nelson, William Nietman, Hank Peck, Monty Poen, Reid Riner, Joseph and Marie Rolle, Douglas and Nancy Rutan, Larry Schnebly, Judith Sellers, Nancy Serenbetz, Robert Trotter, Karen Underhill, Thomas Vanderhoof, Douglas Wall, John Wettaw, David Wharton, Clifford White, Linda Whittaker, James R. Wick, Brian Wood, Craig Wood, and Kate Woodman.

NOTES ON THE ORGANIZATION OF THE BOOK

~

A book of this type is always a work in progress. Seeking to make all of the information accurate and current is no easy task, with so many buildings and more than one hundred years to cover. We hope everyone who reads and examines this book will enjoy the fruits of our labor. History is an imperfect discipline and we encourage the reader to provide us with emendations and additional information.

A few notes regarding format and style will assist those who read the book. The older photographs vary in quality and definition. The good folks at Cline Library did a superb job of scanning these at the highest possible resolution. When attempting to photomatch older photographs of campus buildings, a variety of factors interfered with camera positions. There are more trees (thankfully) than sixty to eighty years ago. In a number of instances, newer buildings now occupy a location that might provide the best photographic perspective of a particular structure. In 2009, there was a significant amount of construction on campus; on some occasions, these efforts blocked what would otherwise have been favorable camera positions. Overall, the process for obtaining current pictures worked quite well and provided many new views of structures.

At the beginning of chapters 1 through 5, there is a brief narrative describing the institutional epoch and the broader historical events that shaped the period. A map and aerial photograph are located at the beginning of these chapters (two maps for chapter 3) highlighting new buildings that appeared during that period. New buildings are delineated in orange. This provides a wonderful picture of the changes that occurred over 110 years. Combining the map with an aerial photograph adds to the reader's ability to visualize the physical development of the campus at each major period in its history.

The current name for a given structure is used in the chronological presentation even though it may have had other names previously. The narrative associated with each building provides an overview of its various names and functions over time. Careful use of the index is highly recommended as a place to locate structures that may bear a different name today than was the case in years past. Many people and programs associated with Northern Arizona University are mentioned at multiple locations throughout the book; here, also, using the index should assist the reader.

Providing exact dates regarding various phases of a new building that was added to the campus infrastructure is subject to interpretation. There are often several dates associated with a building's construction and to be exact is not possible given the nature of the records. Dates that do appear in various sources start with planning stages, followed by hearing and appropriation dates at the state legislature in Phoenix. The funding leads, in most cases, to dates for groundbreaking, construction, and completion. Finally, there are dates for the opening of a building, for its occupancy, and for its dedication. There are also instances where funding is appropriated and the building was not constructed at that time (or ever) and perhaps the money was used for another purpose.

Another source of confusion revolves around the many student residence facilities on campus. Changes for gender, class year, and such designations as honors dorms often shifted yearly. This becomes extremely difficult to follow as the number of dorms increases, beginning in the 1960s. Thus, we mention some aspects of occupancy but, largely, have not attempted to record, on a regular basis, this sort of information.

Finally, throughout the book, we avoid using names of current or recent faculty or staff. To do so, even on a minor scale, could result in hurt feelings and would require unfair judgments concerning which names to use or not use. Exceptions, of course, occur for individuals for whom a building is named.

Each of us carries different recollections of places and events and what we experienced is subject to both varying interpretations and the vagaries of time. Thus, we beg your indulgence and again ask that you assist this effort by providing us with corrections, alternative information, and any additional pieces of the puzzle that you would care to add. To facilitate this, we have inserted a brief section called "Unsolved Mysteries" in the back-matter essay "Building Northern Arizona University."

NOTES ON MAPS AND AERIAL PHOTOGRAPHS

∾

Seven maps of the Northern Arizona University campus are placed at intervals throughout the book. Each of the five main chapters has a map and, where available, a complementary aerial photograph. For the period 1957–1979, when major additions occurred to the university's physical plant, there are two maps (but only one aerial), splitting the twenty-two-year span roughly in half. There is also an outline map for the campus roads, in chapter 6.

Two templates were used for the maps: one for the first half of the book, through the middle of chapter 3 and covering the period 1899–1967, and a second template for 1967–2008, covering the rest of chapter 3 through chapter 6. In the appendix at the back of the book there is an alphabetical listing of buildings with map key number and page number. The building numbering system is that of the current (2008) scheme at Northern Arizona University. For earlier buildings that were not numbered in this scheme, we started with number 101 and went up to 115.

To aid the reader in picturing the changes on campus over time, those structures that are new for a given time interval are highlighted in orange on each map. In this way, it is possible to follow the growth of the university and to visualize those buildings added during each particular interval.

An aerial photograph was selected to match roughly the date of each map, except for the second map (1979) in chapter 3, for which no aerial was available. Combining the aerial photograph with its map provides a full picture and perspective on campus development through time.

INTERPRETING THE NORTHERN ARIZONA UNIVERSITY LANDSCAPE

CLUES TO THE AMERICAN SCENE

THOMAS PARADIS

During the 1970s, an insightful cultural geographer proclaimed that our entire human landscape—that is, everything we have built and created for ourselves—could be "read" like a textbook. To use his own words, Peirce Lewis taught that "our human landscape is our unwitting autobiography, reflecting our tastes, our values, our aspirations, and even our fears, in tangible, visible form" (Lewis 1979, 12). To unleash some larger meaning of the campus scene at Northern Arizona University (NAU), then, is to reveal some of the ways in which a local university can provide a wealth of visual clues about how our national values and interests have played out through the years. A brief examination of NAU's own historical growth and development trends should well illustrate this point.

Since colonial times, American college campus landscapes have followed an ideal that is traceable to medieval English universities. The idea of being "collegiate" reflected the practice of living and studying together in "small, tightly regulated colleges" (Turner 1984, 3). This college-as-community model contrasted with that of continental Europe, where students' extracurricular activities outside of academic studies were of little importance. Even Thomas Jefferson, primary designer of the University of Virginia campus in 1817, voiced his plan to encourage an "academical village" (Turner 1984, 3). Through the centuries, then, American university design and layout continue to follow the English medieval precedent of creating self-sufficient communities. As with NAU, such internal community engagement emerges through the standard offerings of recreational facilities, sports arenas, dining halls, student housing, and social venues.

Though its precedents began in medieval England, NAU demonstrates some uniquely American attributes. It was early Americans who began to place nascent campuses primarily within rural settings, as opposed to the urban campus tradition of England. A distinctly American ideal of a "college in nature" prevailed, given popular notions that learning should take place in settings "removed from the corrupting forces of the city" (Turner 1984, 4). Of course, larger campuses have become virtual cities in themselves, striving toward some degree of self-sufficiency. Reflecting this rural ideal, or perhaps because of it, campuses such as that of NAU have been designed with low-density open-ness and expansiveness in mind. Though densely clustered American campuses certainly exist, they are the exception. NAU better represents the norm, with isolated buildings set within a milieu of scenic open space. Students and faculty continue to both admire and scoff at such expansiveness each year when struggling to find efficient routes between North Campus and South Campus. The word "campus" itself reflects this pastoral, anti-urban ideal infused deeply within American culture, promoting the idea of "college as countryside." The term "campus" was first used in its strict Latin meaning for "a field," referring to the green, expansive grounds of Princeton and other American universities in place by the late 1700s. NAU's own pastoral campus is consequently a product of such eastern precedents.

Given these general comments on campus layout and planning, it may be useful to understand NAU's historical development through the broad lens of architectural styles and trends. In this context, it is reasonable to identify five overlapping periods of architectural development on the Flagstaff campus since its beginning in 1899. As a southwestern university, NAU was a late bloomer compared to many of its eastern and midwestern counterparts. Construction of the first campus building, Old Main, coincided with America's last full decade of Victorianism, which provided one of the most expressive, opulent, and eclectic architectural periods in our history. New technologies, mass production, and rail transportation all resulted from America's booming Industrial Revolution, referred to less enthusiastically by Mark Twain as the Gilded Age. Though national enthusiasm for Victorian architectural styles such as Queen Anne, Italianate, Romanesque Revival, and French Second Empire was waning in the East at the time of Old Main's construction, the largely rural West retained interest in Victorianism for an additional decade. It should come as no surprise, then, that Old Main's dominant architectural style of Romanesque Revival reflects the final gasp of America's Victorian era, which had spanned six decades. National tastes were shifting, and NAU's intersection with Victorianism did not go beyond construction of its first building.

The second phase of development at NAU is identified through a collection of buildings on North Campus, representing the first three decades of growth that focused on Old Main as a centerpiece. Though nodding to the Victorianism of that first structure, newer buildings highlighted evolving national trends in architectural tastes. The Chicago Columbian Exposition had come and gone by 1894 but left in its wake a powerful architectural impetus that lasted until World War II. The exposition's "White City" inspired architectural firms and civic leaders to adopt a revival of formal classicism, whereby monumental railway, civic, and religious buildings sought to replicate the classical columns, temples, and ornamentation reminiscent of ancient Greece and Rome.

Complete with the connotations of Greek democracy and education, this neoclassical style of architecture was irresistible to college leaders and architects. Though the Flagstaff campus was still small and growing slowly, the neoclassical movement remains quite visible throughout North Campus. Most prominent is Blome Building, with its thick, Tuscan columns and imposing, temple-front portico. More subtle are the pilasters (flat columns) and classical ornamentation embedded into numerous neighboring buildings. Adding to this theme of classicism were other "period" styles also popular at the time, such as

Italian Renaissance, Georgian, and Colonial Revival. Still, these earlier structures continued to sport the same red, Moenkopi sandstone as a primary construction material, providing to this day a uniform sense of place.

A two-decade slumber during the Depression and World War II followed this second phase of campus growth. With peacetime and economic growth, however, came an ensuing baby boom and the GI Bill, two powerful forces that shaped American education for decades to follow. The Arizona State College at Flagstaff, as NAU was named after 1945, went along for the wild ride of student population growth and ensuing campus expansion to meet the increasing demand for higher education. A third phase of campus development was under way, though by this time national sentiment no longer favored historical precedents to inspire its architecture. Instead, this budding, postwar "modern" era was characterized by distinct rejection of the past and growing enthusiasm for anything that represented economic and social progress, technology, and modernization. Architects took their cue as well, having provided early examples of modern, nonhistorical designs during the early twentieth century before their flowering ideas were cut off by two decades of stagnation. During those early years, the concept of history itself had already become resented in Europe for "binding men to antiquated institutions, ideas, and values" (Lowenthal 1985, 379).

With the Depression and war behind them, however, architectural modernism could now flourish on both sides of the Atlantic. Middle-class, suburban lifestyles during the 1940s–1970s became increasingly utilitarian, antihistoric, and functional. Two of the most prominent building types came to symbolize this modernism—namely, the cookie-cutter ranch houses of our new automobile suburbs and the ever-taller "glass box" high-rises dominating urban skylines. Such building forms were considered progressive, given

the belief that only original, new architectural styles could adequately express society's fascination with the future.

What emerged to become perhaps the most dominant architectural style in American history was the so-called International style. Actually not a "style" at all, the point of these modern glass-and-brick cubes was pure functionalism on their interiors while rejecting any hint of exterior styling based on historical precedents. College campuses were not immune to this architectural wave, and NAU was no exception. Through the prototype boxy, glass-and-steel structures designed by such modern architects as Ludwig Mies van der Rohe and Eliel Saarinen, the International style swept the United States and dominated civic and corporate architecture for some four decades. One particular design of "Miesian" architecture, Crown Hall, built in 1956 at the Illinois Institute of Technology, set the trend for future campus architecture. Crown Hall provided a functional, rational approach to building design focused on a structure dominated by steel and plate glass. Coincident with the rapid expansion of NAU, it is no surprise that the International style dominated new building construction through much of the central and south parts of campus. Today the architecture of modernism remains prominent throughout NAU and nearly omnipresent south of Old Main. Perhaps stylistically unappealing to many, NAU's "International-style" campus becomes more meaningful when we learn something of the national ideals and attitudes that shaped it.

An ill-defined fourth period of development at NAU is best characterized as a transition from the third, modernist period. The highlight was the emergence of a physically separated "South Campus" of NAU, invoking a creative educational idea of the 1960s termed the "cluster campus." NAU officials visited cluster campuses elsewhere to learn of their potential. Reflecting America's continued anti-urban sentiments, the primary goal of the cluster campus concept was to reduce dense concentrations of students. The result at NAU was eight major buildings comprising a suite of community functions including a small administration building, student union, dining hall, heating plant, and classroom, research, office, and library buildings. The architecture of the buildings still relied heavily on the International style of modernism, but with an important twist. Many of their facades exhibited tapered walls of brick that expand outward toward their foundations, "suggestive of the great pre-Columbian civilization of Central America" (Cline 1999, 306). Their collective design reflected a national trend of retreating gradually from the "anonymous glass box" of strict modernism toward a hint of historical allusion. The uniformity of the South Campus plan, therefore, provides a glimpse of early postmodernism, a reaction to modernism that would only increase in intensity throughout the late twentieth century.

A fifth and ongoing period of NAU development is likewise mirroring national patterns. By the 1990s, civic and domestic architecture entered into a full-blown postmodern period of urban design that shows no signs of abating. Associated with a return toward historical styles and ornamentation is the "new-urbanism" movement, tagged as such by architects and urban planners encouraging more pedestrian- and environmentally friendly urban settings that deemphasize the automobile. By 2008, architectural variety and urban infill were slowly replacing the modernist tenants of functionality and sprawl. NAU leadership has embraced these new-urbanist ideals since the 1990s, providing the most recent opportunity to interpret the local campus

scene as an indicator of larger, national trends. With little room to spread outward, NAU has instead focused inward, reclaiming expansive parking lots in favor of new buildings and green spaces. Since 1990 the urban density of NAU has increased, with infill projects too numerous to mention here. Some earlier signature projects included the Cline Library addition and the Recreation Center, with more recent additions including McKay Village, Aspen Crossing Learning Community, and the Applied Research and Development (ARD) Building. Many of these structures exhibit fully postmodern facades, featuring combinations of curvilinear and angular shapes and orientations (the ARD, W. A. Franke College of Business Administration, and renovated Engineering and Technology Buildings) or alluding to specific historical styles once again. Cases representing this latter trend include the McKay Village complex, which embraces the national revival of Craftsman Bungalow architecture, and—earlier—the Cline Library addition on Central Campus with its contemporary version of a neoclassical facade and entryway.

In these ways, postmodern architecture and the new-urbanism movement have arrived and will no doubt continue to inform the campus landscape. Peirce Lewis's description of the human landscape as our society's "unwitting autobiography" remains true today. A stroll through the dynamic NAU campus can reveal much about historical values, architectural trends, and contemporary interests and priorities. Readers are encouraged to "light out for the territory" and look at it, as America's historical progression of interests, tastes, and values are all right there for us to see.

NORTHERN ARIZONA UNIVERSITY

A BRIEF INTRODUCTION

Northern Arizona Normal School (NANS) opened its doors in the fall of 1899. The processes associated with establishing the school involved a series of interesting circumstances, thoroughly covered in the existing histories of Northern Arizona University (NAU). The Arizona Territory authorized construction of a reform school for boys between the ages of eight and eighteen. Several tracts of land, totaling 130 acres, were purchased from the railroad as a site for the reform school. By early 1897, territorial lawmakers decided that the unfinished building in Flagstaff would best serve as a branch of the "hospital for the insane" in Phoenix. When that plan did not materialize, the 1899 territorial legislature concluded that a need for instructors for schoolchildren would provide a suitable use for the building. Thus was hatched a plan to use the building as a teacher training institution.

What became Northern Arizona University was born as an institution for educating the teachers who would go forth to the various areas of the state to provide schooling for young people in primary and secondary grades. The seed structure for this endeavor, now called Old Main, grew and matured into a campus that today has almost one hundred extant structures. Of course, along the way, many buildings have come and gone; progress has a way of taking down the old and building up the new.

The book is arranged primarily in chronological order, with a few exceptions where two or three structures, built separately through time, merged into a single building today or shared a similar function. For each building, there is a brief synopsis of the construction, its occupants, and its purpose through the decades and information on the architecture and any significant renovations that took place. Included for all buildings named after people, living or deceased, are a photograph and brief biography. In this way, by providing a short text on each building to accompany pictures of that structure, and where appropriate an associated biography, the whole will comprise a different sort of history of Northern Arizona University. All buildings have stories to tell. We have included a number of these anecdotes for many buildings.

The school at Flagstaff went through a series of name changes as it grew and expanded. It was Northern Arizona

Normal School (NANS) from 1899 to 1925 and then North-ern Arizona State Teachers College (NASTC) from 1925 to 1929. Named Arizona State Teachers College at Flagstaff (ASTCF) for sixteen years, from 1929 to 1945, it became Arizona State College at Flagstaff (ASCF), also called Arizona State College (ASC), from 1945 to 1966. From 1966 to the present, it has been Northern Arizona University (NAU). We use these abbreviations throughout the book.

From an initial enrollment of just twenty-three students for the inaugural class in 1899, the student population has grown to more than twenty thousand. At the same time, the faculty increased from two to more than eight hundred. Supporting students and faculty are more than eight hundred staff. If those who were part of NANS early in the twentieth century could return today, they would be amazed at the size of the institution. They would be thrilled with the fact that the core mission has both retained its original focus and expanded with changes in society, ensuring that NAU remains a leader in meeting the needs of our region, state, and nation.

ABBREVIATIONS, NAU NAME CHANGES, AND NAU PRESIDENTS

Abbreviations

ABOR	Arizona Board of Regents
ASC	Arizona State College
ASCF	Arizona State College at Flagstaff
ASTCF	Arizona State Teachers College at Flagstaff
NANS	Northern Arizona Normal School
NASTC	Northern Arizona State Teachers College
NAU	Northern Arizona University

NAU Name Changes

1899–1925	Northern Arizona Normal School (NANS)
1925–1929	Northern Arizona State Teachers College (NASTC)
1929–1945	Arizona State Teachers College at Flagstaff (ASTCF)
1945–1966	Arizona State College at Flagstaff (ASCF), Arizona State College (ASC)
1966–present	Northern Arizona University (NAU)

NAU Presidents

1. Almon Taylor (NANS, 1899–1909)
2. Rudolph Blome (NANS, 1909–1918)
3. Guy Cornelius (NANS, 1918–1919)
4. John Creager (NANS, 1919–1920)
5. Lynn McMullen (NANS, 1920–1925)
6. Fassett Cotton (NASTC, 1925–1926)
7. Grady Gammage (NASTC and ASTCF, 1926–1933)
8. Thomas Tormey (ASTCF, 1933–1944)
9. Tom Bellwood (ASCF, 1945–1947)
10. Lacey Eastburn (ASCF, 1947–1957)
11. J. Lawrence Walkup (ASCF and NAU, 1957–1979)
12. Eugene Hughes (NAU, 1979–1993)
13. Clara Lovett (NAU, 1993–2001)
14. John Haeger (NAU, 2001–present)

NORTHERN ARIZONA UNIVERSITY

THE FORMATIVE YEARS

Northern Arizona Normal School (NANS) opened in the fall of 1899, with two faculty members and twenty-three students. Early years involved a training program of courses to prepare teachers to instruct the youth of the Arizona Territory. To teach in public schools, one needed a certificate. A student could take a four-year high school program at NANS, with the fourth year devoted to pedagogy and practice teaching. Students who finished a four-year high school program could attend NANS to complete a required year of courses and practice teaching. A four-year high school curriculum offered at NANS prepared students for admission to universities.

The first president, Almon Taylor, oversaw expansion from one building (Old Main) to three, adding two dormitories—Taylor and Bury Halls. NANS's second president, Rudolph Blome, presided over further expansion, including two dormitories, Morton and Campbell Halls, the Hanley Dining Hall, and the heating plant. The Ashurst Building opened as the first community hall on campus. Blome, forced from office during World War I, gave way first to Guy Cornelius and then John Creager, each serving less than two years. Lynn McMullen, the fifth president, aided campus landscaping, including the stone wall on North Campus.

During the 1920s, several buildings appeared; only a few of these remain. The new teacher training building was dedicated to Rudolph Blome in 1983, to honor his devotion to NANS. Collapsible Summer Cottages made their debut to accommodate students during summer sessions. The college started a small dairy farm in 1923; this lasted until the late 1930s.

Fassett Cotton was president of the college from 1925 to 1926; the gymnasium (Riles Building) opened during his tenure. Grady Gammage served from 1926 to 1933, when he became president of that other school (Arizona State University) in Tempe. One new building appeared during the Gammage years, the Open Forum House, completed in 1931.

Thomas Tormey served as president from 1933 until he joined the Civilian Defense Coordinating Council in 1943. During his tenure, construction of North Hall completed a quadrangle of residences for women. A series of stone dwellings, known as Cottage City, was constructed from 1938 to 1940.

Tom Bellwood, a faculty member and administrator, became president for two years near the conclusion of World War II (1945–1947). Returning soldiers, taking advantage of the GI Bill, necessitated assembling temporary

structures for housing, offices, and instruction. In 1945, paved campus streets replaced dirt and rock paths.

In the first five years, costs amounted to $190 per year, including the $20 tuition fee. By 1925, the annual cost was $251, with tuition eliminated for in-state students. By 1947, the cost of tuition, room, and board totaled $435 per year, with no tuition charge for in-state students.

The college's sole mission was producing teachers for

schools in Arizona. Like many normal schools in the United States, the Flagstaff institution began changing after World War II. Alterations of teacher preparation programs, shifting societal needs, technological discoveries and innovations spawned by the war, and other factors melded together, influencing American higher education. Many normal schools underwent progressive change, with some becoming comprehensive colleges and universities.

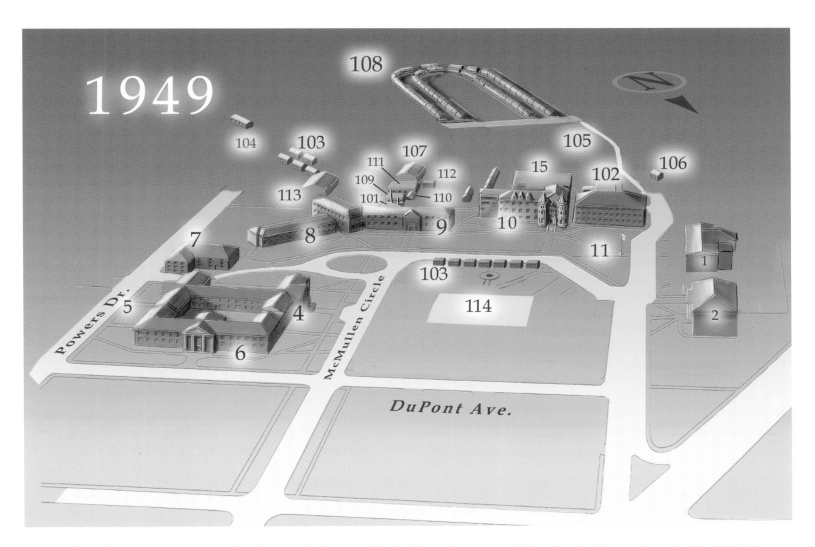

The map (1949) and aerial photograph (1946) depict the location of the buildings that comprised the college in the years just after World War II. Though the photograph and map are not from exactly the same year, together they represent the campus as it appeared in 1946–1949, matching chapter 1 of the text and ending around the time the presidency of Lacey Eastburn began. The growth of the campus to this point was confined to the area known today as the Historic North Campus District and a few ancillary buildings, most of which are now gone from the campus. Comparing the map and photograph gives an overall view of the college as it looked for much of its first forty years.

(A key for building numbers is on page 301.)

Old Main

Old Main, the first building on campus, emerged in stages between 1894 and 1899. Initially, the building was to house a reform school for wayward boys from northern portions of the territory. This use, as well as the suggestion of using it as a facility for the mentally impaired, was abandoned after failing to gain support from the territory and town. The partially completed building lay dormant until 1898, when it became the first building for the newly approved Northern Arizona Normal School (NANS). The first classes convened in September 1899.

Constructed in the Richardsonian Romanesque style, its prominent features include parapeted dormers extending above the roofline, twin "towers" with conical roofs, and heavy stone arches above some windows. The structure was built with locally quarried Moenkopi sandstone, also used in downtown Flagstaff structures of that period. Old Main sits on a small knoll with views of the North Campus area.

Old Main was the sole academic building for several decades, housing a library, administration offices, and classrooms and laboratories. The President's Office was in Old Main for many years, moving eventually to the Gammage Building. The campus assembly hall was on the second floor. The first purchase for the library was two Webster's dictionaries from Montgomery Ward in Chicago. The building housed portions of the institutional administration and served as a dormitory for men from 1963 to 1984. Current occupants include the Alumni Office, the NAU Foundation, art galleries and museum, and University Advancement.

During World War II, Arizona State Teachers College at Flagstaff participated in Navy V-12 training; the first floor of Old Main served as the program's administrative offices. Old Main became a men's residence in 1963 when the student population outpaced construction of new dormitories. The 1976 renovations, carried out while students remained in the dormitory fighting dust and noise, suffered delays due to vandalism, as well as repeated thefts of cement blocks.

Other renovations to Old Main occurred over the years. The first happened as the school opened, alterations to modify space for the Training School. J. C. Grim performed the work for $700. Grim was later a member of the Board of Education for NANS and his son was among the first male graduates. A 1928 renovation included adding two floors to the east wing, with classrooms and a library reading room. A new "modern" gas plant for the building was based on a mixture of gasoline and air—a potentially explosive combination. A collection of used whisky bottles in the attic serves as a reminder of the building's service as a men's dormitory.

An unplanned renovation took place during the summer of 1934 when Dr. Charles Hablutzel, of the science faculty, was preparing a chemistry demonstration with flash powder in the basement. An explosion shattered windows in the labs and lecture halls, as well as demolishing desks and other equipment. In 1950, with the arrival of the first campus-wide telephones, the FOX telephone service provided fifty-seven lines for $200 a month, with the base system located in Old Main.

Several times, officials considered demolishing Old Main or part of it, to make room for new construction, such as a liberal arts building, or to avoid costs associated with renovations. Old Main survived these deliberations and joined the National Register of Historic Places in 1986. Old Main and the Ashurst Building were connected in 1991.

*An "A" over the main entrance
to Old Main signifying Arizona
State College (1950s).*

Trees and landscaping add to the wonderful architecture of Old Main (2008).

Taylor Hall

The first student dormitory at NANS opened in 1905 and was initially referred to as Girls' Dormitory, then changed to Boys' Dormitory in 1908 with the completion of Bury Hall. Renamed Taylor Hall in 1920, the building's construction was funded by an allocation of $10,000 from the territorial legislature. Original construction involved minimalist Victorian features that nodded to the Romanesque Revival architecture of Old Main, while also including a neoclassical porch and symmetrical front facade. The structure represented a transition from the late Victorian era to a more diverse era of "period" styles during the early twentieth century. After additions and renovations, the current architecture is more similar to the characteristics of neoclassical style as evidenced in the rectangular pattern of the brick entryway and the pilasters on the east wing facade.

Taylor Hall's first major modification occurred in 1915, with wings added on both sides of the original structure. In 1935, another two-story wing was added, and the building was covered with brushed, red-sandstone-colored concrete. Taylor Hall has remained a men's dormitory since 1908. During World War II, it was home for U.S. Navy personnel as part of the V-12 unit on campus.

Until the 1960s, all dormitories on campus had head residents or a family living in an apartment in the building. For example, Joe and Marie Rolle served as residents for Taylor Hall from 1947 to 1953. It was customary to hold a room inspection once each week; students were required to have their rooms clean and organized, with the bed made and clothing stored properly. Those out of compliance paid a small fine. At Taylor Hall, the Rolles collected these fines, using them to provide doughnuts in the dormitory entry hall, with Sunday tea and coffee. The names of the young men who contributed to the fund for that week were on a bulletin board above the table containing the doughnuts.

For several years, beginning in 1947, one first-floor room served as a student store, selling sundries such as gum, magazines, soaps, razors, cigarettes, and Lumberjacks T-shirts. Another first-floor room housed a billiards table. One tradition, which lasted for more than fifteen years during the late twentieth century, was an annual Halloween Haunted House. Students and townspeople toured through a terror-filled labyrinth.

Biography

Almon Nicholas Taylor was born on November 1, 1855, at Portland, New York. His father was a grape farmer who died when Almon was seven. Taylor attended high school at Sherman, New York; he worked to pay his room and board. He earned a baccalaureate degree in classical studies from the University of Michigan at Ann Arbor, and a law degree in 1882 at the same institution. He practiced law at Buffalo, New York, for a year before returning to Sherman, New York, as school superintendent. Taylor also served as superintendent at Westfield and Jamestown, New York.

In 1898, Almon Taylor was recruited to become the first principal (president) of the new normal school at Flagstaff.

Almon Taylor, first president of Northern Arizona Normal School.

He came to town, intending to remain for two years, but stayed until 1909. In 1901, he obtained his doctorate from Arkansas Normal College (a community center in Jamestown, Arkansas), via correspondence courses. Eventually, he retired to a grape farm back in Westfield, New York, where he died on October 17, 1937.

His legacy as the first president of NANS includes establishing the teacher training program, development of a modest library collection, and the politics of keeping NANS in operation. Considerable sectionalism in Arizona at the time made it necessary to defend the need for a teacher training program in the northern portion of the territory.

Taylor Hall several years after completion (ca. 1908), with male residents standing in front of the building.

An expanded and modified Taylor Hall in about 1940, with considerable vegetation and altered front entrance.

Modern view of Taylor Hall with portico, porch, and front steps removed. Visible in the left rear of the photograph is the top of the New Laboratory Facility.

Bury Hall

Bury Hall opened on October 2, 1908, as a women's dormitory; Taylor Hall became the men's dormitory. Like Taylor Hall, Bury involved a mixture of neoclassical and late Victorian architectural features. A 1944 photo shows a full-length neoclassical porch with double columns, and Romanesque Revival gables similar to the central gable of Taylor Hall. In this way, the campus was "updating" its architecture to be in step with the times while nodding to the late Victorian flair of Old Main for architectural consistency. Several renovations and modifications to the original structure occurred over time. The first renovation, in 1930, involved adding several new dormers to the second-floor roofline. The second renovation of Bury Hall, in 1950, involved removal of the front porch and several dormers on the second story, while adding a new, modest entrance. Later, a postwar International-style entryway was constructed with Roman bricks.

The history of Bury Hall as a dormitory involves several notes. The building served male students for most of its years; however, in 1925, it was partitioned, so the west end housed males and the east end housed females, making Bury Hall the school's first coeducational dormitory. In 1929–1930, the building again became exclusively a men's dormitory. The basement of the original structure contained a large cafeteria, intended for use by students who lived off campus; these were the first commuter students. Bury Hall remained a men's dormitory until 2001, when NAU converted it to office space. Bury Hall is currently occupied by the Academic Information Office and portions of the university's administrative computing systems.

Biography

Frances (Fanny) Bury joined the NANS faculty at its inception as an assistant to Almon Taylor and as one of the first two instructors, at a salary of $110 per month. She had previously been a faculty member at the Tempe Normal School. She and Taylor traveled by horse and buggy throughout the northern portions of the territory, recruiting students to the first class. Frances Bury taught English, drawing (art), and arithmetic. She also directed the student-organized Mandolin Club. In 1906, Bury married Eugene A. Sliker, treasurer of the Arizona Lumber and Timber Co. and left her position at NANS after seven years on the faculty. Eugene Sliker later became a member of the NANS Board of Education.

Frances Bury, one of the first two instructors at NANS.

A pre-1920 view of Bury Hall, with its long front porch.

A view of Bury Hall (1944) showing several modifications, particularly additional dormers and significant plant growth, which characterized the building by 1940.

Bury Hall (2007), without the porch or vegetation.

Hanley Hall *(No Longer Standing)*

Built as a dining hall in the Craftsman Bungalow style in 1912, Hanley Hall went through many changes during its existence. After serving as a dining facility for more than two decades, the structure changed in 1936–1937 to house the science departments, relocated from Old Main.

Soon after the science departments moved to Frier Hall in 1948, Hanley Hall became a men's dormitory. For several years in the mid-1960s, the basement of Hanley Hall housed laboratories for biology. After its use as a dormitory ended in 1999, alterations were made to accommodate new occupants, including the Center for Sustainable Environments; the Quaternary Studies Program; the Merriam-Powell Center for Environmental Research; the Institute for Tribal Environmental Professionals (ITEP); the Community, Culture, and Environment Program; and the Colorado Plateau Cooperative Ecosystem Studies Unit.

The Hanley Hall dining facility replaced the earlier one in the basement of Bury Hall. The dining area had just twelve tables; all meals were served with linen tablecloths and napkins and students wore what would now be considered business attire. At times, when enrollment growth surged, Mother Hanley and her crew served five meals a day, essentially a continuous service to accommodate student needs.

NAU razed Hanley Hall in the summer of 2005, in preparation for construction of the New Laboratory Facility that occupies the site of the former Dining Hall, Science Building, dormitory, and office space. A significant portion of the exterior stonework of Hanley Hall was preserved and incorporated into portions of the exterior walls and capstones on the east side of the new building. A memorial to Mother Hanley is located on the eastern edge of the Old Campus, near the laboratory facility.

Biography

Margaret Ann "Mother" (Murphy) Hanley was born on November 26, 1874, in Denver, Colorado. She married Patrick Hanley and together they had three children. During some of her forty-one years as head of dining hall operations, the family lived on the third floor of the building later named for her. Eventually they moved to a house purchased in 1920, located across Dupont Street from Campbell Hall and Hanley Hall.

Mother Hanley is among the most beloved of all people associated with NAU. She began as the person in charge of the dining area in Bury Hall, and moved to the new structure upon its completion in 1912. She was in charge of dining facilities, in various capacities and with various titles, including superintendent of dining halls, for forty-one years. She began when President Blome was in office and worked under seven different administrations, concluding with President Eastburn. She was twice voted the homecoming dedicatee, was honored by the students on each Mother's Day, and served as homecoming queen for 1936.

Mother Hanley, in the early 1950s near the time of her retirement, working in one of the kitchens she managed for more than four decades.

Mother Hanley worked with a quiet, but effective style, achieving success with students who performed various tasks in the dining facilities. Her tenure was sufficiently long that she regularly supervised the sons and daughters of those who had earlier worked for her. During World War II, Mother Hanley played a major role in providing dining services for the Navy personnel on campus. For the winter holidays in 1946, she was treated to her first airplane trip, a journey first to Phoenix and then to Yuma, to be with family and friends. She retired from what had become Arizona State College at Flagstaff in 1953, at age seventy-nine, and died on January 29, 1955, at St. Joseph's Hospital in Phoenix.

Hanley Hall as a dining hall in its original Craftsman Bungalow style.

Major alterations to Hanley Hall in the 1930s shroud the earlier structure.

Original Power and Heating Plant

(No Longer Standing)

The original campus power and heating plant, constructed in 1913, served until 1950. It remained as an auxiliary backup for the new plant for several years. The original structure, constructed of sandstone blocks, had two smokestacks approximately forty feet high. The school purchased a team of horses in 1914 to haul wood fuel to the heating and power plant, and to serve as instructional aids in the agriculture programs. The school had train tracks laid to expedite delivery of wood from nearby mills; these were removed in 1934. In 1931, the plant shifted from wood to coal as fuel, burning approximately 2,200 tons of coal annually. An automatic stoker was installed in 1934 to feed the coal into a new boiler.

Several stories pertaining to the power plant are instructive of life at the college. Each morning, the power plant whistle awakened students. In 1947, the whistle fell silent, a state of affairs that lasted for only three weeks, when repairs were completed and the wake-up whistle resumed. During the years that wood slabs were used as fuel, many tons of sawdust were also transported to campus for fuel. Renovations carried out in 1942 included a conveyor belt system for removing the coal ash from the plant. Unfortunately, a wartime shortage of rubber led to abandonment of the conveyor belt and ash removal by hand continued.

Opposite, left: Demolition of the power plant (1951)—first smokestack falls. Note Lumberjack Gym visible on the right.

Opposite, right: Second smokestack falls. A new heating plant, built in 1949, rendered the old structure obsolete.

Front view of the first heating and power plant. The car suggests the image was taken about 1920.

Morton Hall

Named for Mary Morton, the dormitory opened in 1918 at the northern edge of campus. It is an amalgamation of architectural styles, with a large, grand entryway and rounded arch with a keystone, and two symmetrical wings facing west. Much of the building evidences a Colonial Revival tradition; however, there are influences of Romanesque elements. In its early years, the main library resided in Old Main, but a separate women's library flourished in what was once the music room on the first floor. A dining facility located in Morton Hall was removed in 1954.

During World War II, the U.S. Navy V-12 unit occupied the building with a canteen, barbershop, and post office. Today, Morton Hall is a women's residence and is part of a combined residential unit, named North Morton Hall. Together with Campbell Hall and the connecting wing between Morton and Campbell Halls, constructed in 1935, the complex became the Women's Quadrangle.

Biography

Mary Morton joined the Northern Arizona Normal School faculty in 1907. She was born on November 26, 1875, in Davenport, Iowa. Morton attended schools in Iowa Falls, the University of Iowa, and the University of Chicago. She taught school at Davis, Iowa, and at several locations in the Midwest. She came to Flagstaff in 1906 to visit a friend, took a teaching position at the Emerson School, and then accepted a position at NANS. While on the faculty, she taught English and headed that department. On November 22, 1909, she married Thomas E. Pollock in Iowa Falls, Iowa; they resided in Flagstaff for nearly three decades.

Together, the Pollocks were most influential in the growing community and exerted significant impact on events at the school. A favorite activity was to host gatherings each year for the new students arriving in Flagstaff. They established a loan fund to aid students in completing their NANS education. Mrs. Pollock served the Episcopal Church, the American Association of University Women, and the Women's Club. She was a member of the local school board for several terms.

T. E. Pollock, a banker, rancher, coal production investor, and politician, served on the local committee that worked with the territorial legislature to obtain the normal school for Flagstaff. He died in 1938 and his wife, Mary Morton Pollock, died on March 13, 1941, in Pasadena, California.

Mary Morton Pollock.

Opposite: Front side of Morton Hall (1935), with recently planted trees.

Morton Hall (2007), from the same perspective as the preceding photo.

Campbell Hall

Originally named Babbitt Hall, Campbell Hall opened in 1916, named in honor of State Senator Hugh Campbell. This dormitory became part of the North, or Women's, Quadrangle by the 1930s with the construction of North Hall. The general architectural style embodies characteristics of the Colonial Revival, a popular period style throughout America from the 1890s through the 1920s. In this case, the neoclassical features of the entryway and portico are blended with the Federal-style doorway and oval rose window. The construction material is primarily Ashlar cut, red (Moenkopi) sandstone.

Renovations occurred in 1920, 1937, and 1951. During 1942–1943, the Navy V-12 unit occupied much of the building. In 1946, Campbell Hall became a men's dormitory for several years to accommodate the significant influx of male students after World War II. In 1967, Campbell Hall was the first honors dormitory at NAU, and continues today as a women's honors dormitory.

Biography

Hugh E. Campbell was born on June 10, 1862, at Cape Jehu, Nova Scotia. After attending schools there, he moved first to Wisconsin in 1880, where he worked in the lumber industry, and soon thereafter to Arizona when he was twenty years old. He was a sheep farmer and part owner of the Campbell, Francis Company, a Flagstaff business,

dealing in sheep and wool. He started in the sheep and wool business as a young man and continued throughout his career, serving as president of the Arizona Wool Growers Association from 1910 to 1923. His sheep holdings, at the time of his death, were among the largest in the West.

Hugh Campbell was a state senator from Coconino County, reelected to the state legislature for nearly ten years. When he died of cancer on July 13, 1923, Fred S. Breen, publisher of the *Coconino Sun* (predecessor to today's *Arizona Daily Sun*) and formerly a member of the state legislature, took his place. Hugh Campbell aided the cause of NANS greatly by securing an appropriation of $250,000 for the 1917–1918 biennium. He was a strong advocate for the institution, ensuring sufficient recognition and funding from the state for its continued existence during the early years when the legislature did not always view NANS as important.

State Senator Hugh Campbell.

Right: Campbell Hall (ca. 1920) soon after it opened as a women's dormitory.

Below: Similar view of Campbell Hall (2008), with significant pine growth.

Ashurst Building

The state made an initial appropriation in 1917 to build a wing for Old Main. The original intent was to construct Old Main with two symmetrical wings, but only the east wing was completed. Thus, some sources consider Ashurst to be the "missing" wing, whereas others note that it was originally a separate building. Construction, completed in 1918, has an architectural style reminiscent of Old Main. Ashurst's hipped roof resembles the Blome Building's and there is one distinct belt course of stone. In its early years, Ashurst was home for all school assemblies, commencement exercises, and gatherings with notable visitors. Before construction of the Ashurst Building, the Orpheum Theatre in downtown Flagstaff hosted larger school functions and events.

A 1952 remodel converted the auditorium to a music hall, with contiguous offices and music practice rooms. At the conclusion of World War II, students raised $2,500 for the purchase of a Hammond electric organ for Ashurst to honor those from the school who lost their lives during the war. During its years as the focal point for college events, it was the venue for readings and performances by such notables as the poet Vachel Lindsay, the writer Carl Sandburg, the novelist Jack O'Connor (who served on the school faculty), the actor Andy Devine, and the musician Sir Harry Lauder. Others who appeared in Ashurst include the actor Charles Laughton; David Rubinoff, a renowned violinist; and, just after World War II, the Trapp Family Singers.

As additional venues for campus events were built during the 1950s, Ashurst remained a valuable home for concerts and speakers. It was the first home for the Flagstaff Symphony Orchestra. Ashurst Auditorium is still an important gathering place for speakers, ceremonies to honor faculty and students, dancing, concerts, movies, and special events.

A renovation in 1954 provided extensive, well-soundproofed spaces for music faculty and student practice rooms, along with refurbishing the main hall—then named Ashurst Music Hall. After a 1989 remodel, a portion of the lower level of Ashurst accommodated office space for the Graduate College and Women's Studies. This renovation included the glass-enclosed connector between Old Main and Ashurst. Other units housed in the Ashurst Building over time included portions of the Theatre and Drama Department, the Flagstaff Summer Festival, and the Arizona Center for Vocational Education.

Biography

Henry Fountain Ashurst was born on September 13, 1874, in a sheep camp near Winnemucca in northern Nevada, during the course of a westward wagon trip. His father traveled from the family home in Missouri to the California gold fields. Soon after Henry's birth, the family moved to Williams, Arizona, and two years later, in 1877, to the Mormon Lake area. Henry worked as a ranch hand at the age of twelve, then attended and graduated from the public schools in Flagstaff. While living in Flagstaff, he performed a number of odd jobs, including a stint as a reporter for the local newspaper and working as a lumberman.

*Ashurst was added to the west side of Old Main in 1918,
as seen on the right side of this photograph (1930s).*

Ashurst graduated from the Stockton Business College in California in 1896 and followed that with studies of law and political economy at the University of Michigan at Ann Arbor. After admission to the bar in 1897, Ashurst began a law practice in Williams, Arizona. That same year, he was elected to the Arizona Territorial Legislature. In the ensuing years, he rose rapidly through the political ranks: first as Speaker of the House (1899), then as a state senator, and as county district attorney for Coconino County from 1905 to 1908. He was a gifted public speaker, admired by all, regardless of their political persuasion. A quote by Ashurst, taken from a local obituary, provides a glimpse into his approach to politics: "The welfare of the United States, and the happiness of our people, does not hang on the presence of Henry F. Ashurst in the Senate. When that realization first came to me, I was overwhelmed by the horror of it, but now it is a source of infinite comfort."

Henry Ashurst, a Democrat, was one of the first two U.S. senators from Arizona. He served for twenty-nine years, until January 1941. During his later years in the Senate, he chaired the Judiciary Committee and was part of the group that championed Franklin D. Roosevelt's plan to enlarge the U.S. Supreme Court. After a stint on the Board of Immigration Appeals, he retired in 1943. In 1959, at age eighty-five, he was the commencement speaker for Arizona State College at Flagstaff, receiving an honorary degree. Henry Ashurst died on May 31, 1962, in Washington, D.C.

Henry Fountain Ashurst, U.S. senator and a major figure in Arizona history.

Ashurst Building (2008).

Blome Building
(Teacher Training School)

The new Training School for Northern Arizona Normal School opened in 1921. The architectural style is neoclassical (a revival of the nineteenth-century Greek Revival, much like Campbell Hall) with a temple-shaped portico, hipped roof, bilateral symmetry, and replicate-like Renaissance Tuscan columns at the entrance. The exterior is block-cut, local Coconino sandstone. The structure, located on a small hill at the northwest corner of campus, sits on the site of the first elementary school in Flagstaff, which opened in 1883. To prepare the location for the new school building, Herrington House was shifted to a location near the rear of Ashurst. The old college laundry building, also used for storage, was razed.

The new building remained as the Teacher Training School until 1957. It became the Journalism Building, with the north end of the first floor used by Journalism and the remainder of the building housing the new program in forestry. In those days, Journalism encompassed what we call public affairs and news services, as well as training students in media writing. Renovations in 1957, 1966, and 1983 coincided with changes in occupants and functions. Starting in the 1970s, the name changed to Student Personnel Building and it housed Student Services, University Services, the Public Information Office, and the Sports Information Office for varying periods. Presaging some current functions, offices for Continuing Education and Summer School occupied space in the Blome Building by the early 1980s. At other times, units housed in the building were the Educational Assistance Center, Risk Management, Campus Safety, and the Ombuds Office. Human Resources

The Teacher Training School (1921) soon after its opening.

resided in the building for several decades before moving to the Centennial Building in 2000.

The structure was renamed the Rudolph H. H. Blome Building, honoring the second president of NANS, in 1983. Today, it houses a number of offices, primarily related to Distance Learning and Statewide Education Programs, as well as the Pattea Conference Room (dedicated to the Native American tribes of Arizona), the Electronic Learning Center (ELC), the Faculty Senate, the Institute for Native Americans, and classrooms. Distance Learning and Statewide Education will soon move to a new structure added to the Communications Building.

Biography

Rudolph Harin Heinrich Blome was born in 1854 at Hoyerhagen, Hanover, Germany. He immigrated to the United States with his family in 1869. He attended high school in Illinois and obtained teacher certificates from Wheaton College and Northwestern College (Northwestern Business College) in Naperville, Illinois, in 1877. Blome taught school for several years, eventually becoming principal of schools for Elmhurst, Illinois, in 1883. In 1890, at the age of thirty-six, he received a bachelor's degree from Illinois State Normal School (Illinois State University).

After a stint as principal for the Rice Collegiate Institute at Paxton, Illinois, he moved his family to Jena, Germany, where he obtained his doctorate, studying education, botany, zoology, and philosophy. His dissertation, completed in 1900 when he was forty-six years old, was written in both German and English. He returned to the United States, settling in Tempe, Arizona, where he taught psychology and philosophy of education. He became director of the Teacher Training School at Tempe (Arizona State University).

Rudolph H. H. Blome, the second president of NANS.

In 1909, the Board of Education hired Blome as the second president of NANS. In addition to his administrative duties, Blome taught classes in ethics, school economy, and school management. He served as president until 1918, during the height of World War I, when paranoia about Germans and Blome's ethnic background as a possible sympathizer led to his ouster by the school's governing body. His loyalty to the United States was strong and students protested his dismissal with assemblies and a strike, but to no avail. Blome later served as principal of Bisbee High School in southern Arizona, and as director of State Vocational Education.

Blome's tenure witnessed several positive developments. He was instrumental in securing funding for the Ashurst Building. He pushed the governing board and legislature for a new Training School, the building that bears his name today. Intercollegiate athletics debuted during his presidency.

Blome retired from his position with the state in 1921 and moved to Pasadena, California, where he died on April 3, 1923.

Blome Building (1950s), with the San Francisco Peaks in the background.

Blome Building (2007) from the same perspective as the first (1921) photo of the building.

Herrington House or
President's House *(No Longer Standing)*

Herrington House, formerly located on the hill where the Blome Building is today, was built in 1904 in the Queen Anne architectural style. A stone foundation supported a wood-frame construction. It was the home of George Herrington, manager of the first electric company in Flagstaff. In 1921, George Dunnock received $500 to move the house, making way for construction of the Teacher Training School. At its new location, southwest of Ashurst, it was remodeled in the Bungalow style and by 1923, a new gabled roof was in place; the old roof shingles were reused as siding for the home. Over time, additions to the building included a dormer, a fireplace, enclosing the front porch, and other renovations, resulting in a fourteen-room house.

The relocated home was to serve as a laboratory for women students in domestic arts classes. However, President Lynn McMullen decided that, rather than spend $10,000 allocated for a new residence for school presidents, he would use a much smaller sum to renovate Herrington House for his family. Prior to that time, school leaders had lived as house parents in dormitories. All subsequent presidents of the institution lived in Herrington House, up to and including, for a time, Lawrence and Lucy Walkup. In 1930, with a growing student population, then president Grady Gammage and his wife shared their home with some students for a time.

In 1959, the Walkups moved to the newly completed President's House. In subsequent years, the older structure was used for a variety of purposes, including the Counseling Center (1959–1979), which name it was given for a time; programs like Upward Bound and the Educational Assistance Center (1979–1981); the NAU Security Division; the Office of Athletics (1981–1983); and last as Property Control (1983–1987). During much of this period, the building was called Old Campus House. In deteriorating condition, likely beyond repair, demolition occurred in 1987, by Twin Hills Construction, at a cost of $35,000.

Herrington House (1980).

Herrington House, positioned by the southwest corner of the Riles Building.

McMullen Wall

President McMullen and a group of NANS students constructed the wall in 1921 using Malpais basalt from quarries near Flagstaff. A portion of the wall remains today as posts between Morton Hall and the North Union and at the corner of Dupont Street and Knoles Drive. The wall has disappeared in stages, most recently during construction of the new High Country Conference Center. Stones removed owing to this recent activity will be incorporated into new masonry work at the Japanese Tea Garden at the southern end of campus. Two other locations on campus bear the name of the fifth president of NANS, Lynn McMullen: a circle in the area of the historic center of the campus and McMullen Field, the first location for outdoor athletics, on the grounds between the Riles Building and the Counseling and Testing Center.

Biography

Lynn Banks McMullen was born in 1875 near Arcadia, Indiana, where he grew up. During his youth, he rated as one of the best young tennis players in the state. He obtained his bachelor of science degree from DePauw University in Greencastle, Indiana, in 1897 and a master's degree from the Teachers College at Columbia University in New York. Following graduation, he taught in the public schools of Indiana, including eleven years in Indianapolis. After a brief time as an instructor at Indiana Normal College (Ball State University) in Muncie, Indiana, he spent ten years at the State Normal School in Valley, North Dakota (Valley

City State University), the last five as president. After one year at the Teacher Training School in Greeley, Colorado (Northern Colorado University), McMullen came to NANS as the fifth president, serving from 1920 to 1925.

McMullen, with the aid of students, did considerable tree planting and landscaping on the campus. On April 15, 1921, they planted more than two hundred trees. The fruits of these efforts are visible today as one strolls beneath the sweeping, deciduous canopies on historic North Campus.

The physical development of the campus during McMullen's presidency was modest and pragmatic. He converted Herrington House to become the home for presidents of the school, saving many thousands of dollars. Another aspect of McMullen's financial acumen involved procurement and use of about fifty Summer Cottages, designed to be collapsible for storage during the winter months. Summer sessions were quite popular, drawing teachers and scholars from a wide geographical range and requiring additional housing. As often happens, the "seasonal" cottages became permanent housing; they were dismantled in stages, with complete removal in the 1960s.

McMullen resigned effective in 1925, after another state budgetary crisis threatened the school's existence. He received a doctorate from Columbia University in 1927. Dr. McMullen became the first president of Eastern Montana College (Montana State University–Billings). He retired in 1945 and died on May 18, 1963, in Polson, Montana.

Lynn B. McMullen served as the fifth president of Northern Arizona Normal School.

Opposite: McMullen Wall (1940s) after an ice storm—the Blome Building is in the foreground and a portion of Gammage Building appears in the background.

Cottage City:
Three Housing Systems

From 1921 through 1948, a series of structures occupied portions of the area between the Communications Building and the Cowden Learning Community. The three sets of buildings, all gone today, were (1) Summer Cottages; (2) Stone Cottages, built prior to World War II; and (3) a series of temporary structures provided by the U.S. government after the end of World War II. Since these units coexisted in time, and were collectively referred to as Cottage City on many occasions, they are grouped together here.

These buildings served married students, during the regular academic school year and for summer terms. Some structures occasionally housed single males or served other university needs. Renovations occurred at different times to upgrade, provide better safety, and refurbish the accommodations.

During the years that these three types of housing structures existed, they had much in common, and inter-acted as a single community. A council represented the group's needs to the college. Issues of importance included speeding cars in the presence of children, overloaded and outdated fuses, and a need for maintenance of interior walls and roofs. The community supported a number of activities and organizations—for example, annual Halloween and Christmas parties, a cooperative food store, and a volunteer firefighters' organization. The *Lumberjack* had a column that ran sporadically, depending on input from the residents, called "Cottage City Chatter." In at least one year, there was an Ideal Housewife contest. Judging was based on home decor, child care, and providing a convenient place for study.

Summer Cottages *(No Longer Standing)*

During the spring of 1921, President McMullen identified a projected housing shortage for the upcoming summer session at NANS. He obtained funding for fifty collapsible wooden cottages. Realizing that fifty cottages would not be enough, he later increased the number to seventy-seven. Each cottage (or cabin) was nine feet by twelve feet with a dirt floor, cot, table, chairs, wood-burning stove, and a screened window opposite the entrance. The cottages, sometimes referred to as Cabin Row, cost $37.50 each to construct and the interior furnishings amounted to $50 per cabin. They collapsed by removing four bolts, and folded for winter storage. There was a single light bulb and water came from communal outside taps. The rental fee of $2 per week, per person, was not only reasonable, but was also sufficient to cover the construction cost in a relatively short time. Some second-generation cabins were twelve feet by four-teen feet and had wood stoves. The only hot water available in Cabin Row was in the shared shower building.

When enrollment increased for the 1930 fall semester, President Grady Gammage had fifteen cottages moved to a location near the gym (Riles Building). These cottages, outfitted with heat, running water, and finished interiors, became part of student housing. With a further increase in enrollment during the 1931–1932 year, he had twenty-eight additional Summer Cottages refurbished for year-round use. Though the Summer Cottages were intended to be a temporary solution, they were never dismantled and were used for many years. The exact demolition date(s) of these structures is unknown, though it likely occurred in stages.

Mother and infant in front of a summer housing unit. The first cottages were erected in 1921.

Initially intended for summer use only, after some minor upgrades many of the units served as living quarters during the entire academic year.

Stone Cottages *(No Longer Standing)*

In late 1938, the campus received word that the Public Works Administration (PWA) had granted $67,900 for construction of fifty two-room cottages. An allocation of $20,000 from the State of Arizona supplemented the PWA grant. During 1939, sixty Civilian Conservation Corps (CCC) employees constructed these units under the direction of Pete Solberg (who introduced skiing to Flagstaff). Each unit, constructed with rock wall exteriors, measured fourteen feet by twenty-five feet and had concrete floors, composition roofs, and running water. Three separate buildings with laundry facilities and showers were part of the overall complex. These structures were arranged in a double row, forming a U-shape, on land used for parking lots 16 and 16A and nearby space on the 2008 campus map. Eventually, there were fifty-four single and twenty-two double apartments, a bathhouse, a laundry, and a central structure in the "U" that served as a study hall and post office, along with housing the only telephone.

Students occupied units beginning in the spring of 1941. During World War II, much of Cottage City housed families of workers at the Navajo Ordnance Depot in Bellemont, ten miles west of Flagstaff. In 1945–1946, the state appropriated funds to remodel the cottages with installation of indoor toilets and showers in each cottage. The cottages provided living quarters for married students, and, on many occasions, younger faculty and their families, for another forty years. In the later years, both the Sculpture Studio and a Psychology Laboratory occupied several of the Stone Cottages. The demise of Cottage City occurred in three stages. Removal of some cottages happened when construction of the North Activity Center (University Union Field House) began in 1964. A majority of the Stone Cottages came down in 1984, with two saved as a memorial to the many years of Cottage City; these disappeared by 1986. Some stones from Cottage City are now part of the rock horseshoe at the Skydome.

Left: View of the Stone Cottages, with the horseshoe curvature of the sidewalk.

Opposite: Stone Cottages in winter with the overhang of Field House.

Federal Temporary Housing (*No Longer Standing*)

At the conclusion of World War II, an influx of veterans, attending college on the GI Bill, pushed existing campus facilities beyond their limits. To provide living quarters for the students, and offices and classrooms for instruction, structures were brought to campus. In July 1946, twenty-five rail cars arrived with the wooden structures in pieces, ready for refabrication. Most structures were formerly U.S. Army barracks from Portland, Oregon, and Vancouver, Washington. The Del Webb Corporation moved the units to campus and assembled them at a cost of $54,000. The units consisted of two two-story buildings, measuring 108 feet by 38 feet, with fourteen apartments in each structure. There were two single-story buildings measuring 96 feet by 50 feet, with eight apartments each, and a building measuring 40 feet by 48 feet, with a single story and four apartments.

By the summer of 1946, an additional thirty-two apartments in four one-story buildings came to campus, courtesy of the Federal Public Housing Authority. Many of these units were located where Raymond Hall and McDonald Hall are today, just east of the Stone Cottages. Together, they were known as Splinter City.

Temporary buildings were located behind Old Main, extending south just east of the Riles Building. At least one structure was on land occupied by the Communications Building. Demolition of the buildings occurred over time as the campus expanded. Many of these structures were associated with Cottage City and are visible on campus maps and aerial photographs (see the beginning of this chapter). Some office and instructional buildings continued in service until the early 1960s. The last wooden structures disappeared by 1965.

Opposite: Mother with baby standing in front of the temporary housing surrounded by winter snow and icicles.

Dairy Barn *(No Longer Standing)*

In 1923, a dairy barn appeared on the NANS campus. This building was just southeast of the campus, approximately where the Home Management House is located, and was built of cut stone quarried locally. The school purchased a small herd of Holstein cows to provide milk for the dining halls and employment for students. An increase in enrollment occurred in 1930 exceeding the school's ability to house the students in residence halls. Creative housing solutions included doubling up the occupancy of dormitory rooms and using office space, the gymnasium, Herrington House, and the Dairy Barn as temporary residential space.

The Depression placed a financial strain on everyone, including the school. In 1932, with forty head of cattle producing 23,500 gallons of milk, 600 pounds of cheese, and 1,300 pounds of meat, the dairy herd saved the college about $2,600 in food costs. In the same year, a freshman from Lakeside, Arizona, brought a dairy cow, named Cordera, to join the herd. The cow produced 15 quarts of milk per day, which he sold to the college and townspeople, providing funding for his education. President Grady Gammage approved a barter system, allowing students to exchange potatoes and other crops for portions of their college costs.

Another tale concerning the Dairy Barn location involves sanitation on campus. It seems that a geologic structure, referred to as the "bottomless pit," existed on the site later occupied by the barn. The pit, a modest distance from the main campus of those days, was about twelve feet lower than the campus area to the north. Thus, all sewage and runoff water readily drained to the hole in the ground. This arrangement ended some time prior to construction of the Dairy Barn, when the entire area was filled in. For those who may be interested, this location roughly corresponds to the present site of Peterson Hall. Perhaps the regular problems with drainage into the basement of Peterson can be traced to this geologic formation?

By the fall of 1940, the dairy was operating at a loss and pasteurized milk was readily available from local sources; the college sold the twenty-nine dairy cattle to a local rancher. Plans for turning the barn structure into a student union never materialized. Plans to use some of the pasture-lands for a nine-hole golf course designed by Jiggs Insley, the alumni secretary at the time, also faltered soon after work on the course commenced. The first, second, and ninth holes were laid out in 1941, with the first tee positioned near the Dairy Barn, which was to be the clubhouse. The nearby milk shed would serve as the caddy shack. As was common in those days, greens were to be of sand and oil. With the outbreak of World War II, these plans were abandoned. The Dairy Barn and milk shed remained until at least the mid-1950s, serving as storage facilities until their demolition.

Dairy Barn (ca. 1930), with Holstein cows scrutinizing the
photographer, and an excellent view of the stonework.

44

Campus Fountain *(No Longer Present)* and Clock

Prior to 1925, a fountain stood north of Old Main. This location afforded excellent views of the San Francisco Peaks and was a gathering place, where students and faculty could go to relax or converse. The small circular outline, where the fountain stood, is visible on the 1956 campus aerial view. When the North Union and Prochnow Auditorium were under construction in 1951, a student, likely with several accomplices, threw sticks of dynamite into the fountain,

blowing it up and breaking windows in surrounding buildings. Earlier that evening, the group traveled up the old road through Oak Creek Canyon, throwing sticks of dynamite into the surrounding forest. Apparently, no major fires resulted from these efforts. The reconstructed fountain served as a planter for many decades. In 1999, NAU installed an old-fashioned four-sided pedestal clock in the circle where the fountain once stood.

Fountain on North Campus (1930s), with the San Francisco Peaks and the Armory in the background.

Today, the same location features a pedestal clock (2008).

McMullen Field *(No Longer Present)*

A series of athletic fields hosted organized sports teams and recreational activities on campus. Created in 1923, McMullen Field was located just south of the gymnasium, where the Communications Building and Counseling and Testing Center are today. Competitions, most notably in football, engaged teams from local high schools and from the state teacher's college in Tempe. The early nickname for the teams from Tempe was the Pedagogues. A track, surrounding the playing area, served for early meets as well as recreation. During World War II, the Navy V-12 unit used the field for drill practice, as well as Skidmore Field, the successor to McMullen Field.

McMullen Field functioned as a site for athletics and recreation until the 1950s. Skidmore Field replaced McMullen Field as the primary site for football games and other athletic contests; however, football practice continued at McMullen Field.

Right: McMullen Field was the first named outdoor athletic facility at Northern Arizona Normal School. In the rear to the left, portions of Old Main and Ashurst are visible. To the right, the power plant can be seen and, behind it, part of Taylor Hall. Since the gymnasium had not been constructed, this photograph must have been taken around 1923 or 1924.

Opposite: McMullen Field with a Navy V-12 unit conducting drill exercises.

Riles Building *(Gymnasium)*

The first indoor athletic facility at NASTC opened in 1926. Originally called the College Gymnasium, it served as a coeducational gymnasium for several decades, until Lumberjack Gym opened in 1951, at which time the men's physical education and athletics moved to the new building. Before construction of the Riles Building, athletic and recreational events happened at venues around town, such as the Armory. The Riles Building is an example of the Georgian or Colonial Revival architectural style, exemplified by the symmetry and the keystone at the top of the main entrance arch.

The gymnasium housed a basketball court and indoor swimming pool in the basement. The latter was the first such facility in northern Arizona. When the pool opened in 1926, all students and faculty were required to buy new swimsuits; wool fibers clogged the filter system.

A balcony, above the basketball court, could seat five hundred people and the upper level had offices for coaches and faculty. In an early basketball game, a barnstorming team defeated the local men's team 25–19; this group was a forerunner of the well-known Harlem Globetrotters.

During World War II, a firing range existed in the building along the west wall. The range served as a training facility for law enforcement and military personnel; however, its origins relate to the desire for an opportunity to practice for hunting season.

At the time Lumberjack Gym opened, the Riles Building became the Women's Gymnasium, with $100,000 in renovations. The gym continued to house women's physical education until the 1970s when the building became a general, utilitarian recreation facility, the Gym Annex.

A major remodel of the building in 1983 converted it from a gymnasium to office and classroom space. Various units housed in the Riles Building include Residence Life and the Arizona Center for Vocational Education Program. Currently, the building houses the Department of Humanities, Arts, and Religion; Office of the Dean for the College of Arts and Letters; and programs affiliated with the College of Education, including the Arizona Center for Vocational Education and Institute for Future Work Force Development. The Northern Arizona Writing Project, AmeriCorps, Peace Corps, Gerontology Institute, and Master of Liberal Studies Program are also located in the Riles Building today.

Biography

Wilson Camanza Riles was born on June 27, 1917, in a sawmill camp in Elizabeth, Louisiana (near Alexandria), and orphaned at a very young age. With assistance from the local church, he graduated from high school in New Orleans. He moved to Flagstaff to be near relatives and his adoptive parents, Leon and Narvia Bryant, who worked with local sawmill operations.

The football team (ca. 1930) with the Riles Building in the background, with "CHARGE" painted on the gymnasium roof. Herrington House is visible on the left.

View of the north side of the Physical Education Building.

Riles enrolled at Arizona State Teachers College, receiving his bachelor's degree in education in 1940. While an undergraduate, he served as secretary for the Lumber and Sawmill Workers Union for a year, during which time he participated in negotiations that secured a 40 percent pay raise for the workers. He also hosted a late-night jazz program on local radio under the name "Doctor Rhythm."

Wilson Riles first taught at McNary, Arizona, a rural logging camp comprised primarily of African Americans; his annual pay was $900 for the 1940–1941 school year. Following his first year of teaching, he married ASTC alumna Louise Phillips. They returned to Flagstaff where both taught at Dunbar High School; the student body was comprised almost entirely of African Americans. After

South side of the Riles Building (2008), with a corner of Ashurst visible on the left.

North-side view of the main entrance to the Riles Building, prior to renovations.

three years of service in the Army Air Force, Riles obtained his master's degree in public school administration from ASTC in 1947, after which he became principal of Dunbar High School in Flagstaff, a position he held until 1954.

Riles began a career in public service in 1954, accepting a position as executive secretary for the Pacific Region of the Fellowship of Reconciliation, a Quaker organization dedicated to peace. The Riles family relocated to Los Angeles. Riles remained the executive secretary until 1958 when he began working for the California Department of Education. He eventually became associate superintendent of public instruction for California. During his tenure with the Department of Education, he initiated programs in early childhood education and special education, providing models soon followed by other states. He was an early and enthusiastic advocate for the use of computers in the classroom.

In 1970, Riles was elected state superintendent of public instruction, becoming the first African American to hold a statewide office in California. He was reelected in 1974 and 1978, but lost a bid for a fourth term in 1982. Riles was appointed as the chair of the U.S. Office of Education Task Force on Urban Education in 1982, serving under three U.S. presidents—Nixon, Ford, and Carter.

Over the course of his distinguished career, Wilson Riles received numerous awards and accolades. In 1973, the NAACP presented him with their highest award, the Spingarn Medal. He received the first Robert Maynard Hutchins Award for outstanding work in education in 1978. In 1979, he received the Distinguished Alumni Award from the American Association of State Colleges and Universities. He was the first recipient of the Alumni Achievement

Award from NAU (1968) and a recipient of the Distinguished Alumni Medallion from NAU (1975). He received an honorary doctor of laws degree at the spring 1976 NAU commencement and was the commencement speaker in 1983. The gymnasium building was renamed the Riles Building in his honor in 1986. He retired from his career in education with state and federal governments in 1982, ran a consulting firm dealing with education for several years, and died on April 1, 1999, in Sacramento, California.

Wilson Riles (right), with President Lawrence Walkup, at about the time Riles received an honorary degree from Northern Arizona University in 1976.

Gammage Building

Northern Arizona Normal School became Northern Arizona State Teachers College in 1925, and the college was completing construction of a building to house the college's library and administrative offices. Construction was completed in 1930 and it was named in honor of departing president Grady Gammage in 1933.

Prior to construction of the Gammage Building, the library was located in Old Main, with 15,400 volumes. The Gammage Building was designed to accommodate future growth, with a maximum capacity of 60,000 volumes. Students and faculty of the college moved the books from Old Main to the new facility shortly after the building dedication on December 14, 1930.

Many features of the building are characteristic of an Italian Renaissance style, exemplified by the original entryway and window. The white corner blocks, called quoins, provide a stylistic emphasis. Like the neoclassical and Colonial Revival styles, Italian Renaissance remained a popular "period" style until the Great Depression. In this case, the two entrances are of different styles. The administration entrance, part of the 1957–1958 addition, exhibits a modern Art Deco flair, while the library entrance is Italian Renaissance. The building is an interesting study in architectural styles from about eighty years ago. Construction slowed because the builder had difficulty obtaining the red sandstone called for in the specifications. The issue was resolved with the substitution of lighter-colored sandstone.

In 1957–1958, a major administration annex was added to the north side of the existing building. Other remodeling occurred in 1966, with a complete overhaul of the mechanical systems, and in 1987 for the addition of an elevator and stairwells. In 2001, the interior was remodeled.

Occupants of the building have been almost as varied as the architecture. Original occupants were the college administrative offices and the library. With the completion of the Cline Library, most of the Gammage Building became administrative and service offices. The first home for Printing and Duplicating was in the Gammage Building. In fact, some university officials were relieved when the new Executive Center opened in the Central Campus area; their offices adjoined this noisy, and sometimes smelly, operation. Until the Babbitt Administrative Center opened in 1976, virtually all aspects of the university administration resided in Gammage.

In earlier years, the campus telephone system, mail operations, and, for a time, the Mathematics Department were housed in Gammage. The college bookstore resided in Gammage until it moved to the North Union in 1951. The Office of Admissions and Office of Career Placement remained in the Gammage Building until they moved to the North Union in the early 1990s. After the library holdings moved to the Cline Library, a portion of the second floor of Gammage was, for much of the 1970s, a faculty club where lunch was available weekdays. Other spaces on the second floor contained cubicles that housed both faculty and teaching assistants. In 2008, the building became home to the Registrar, Bursar, Comptroller, Travel, Accounts Payable, and Financial Compliance and Audit units. In 2005, Purchasing moved from Gammage to the ROTC/Property Control Building near the Atmospheric Research Observatory.

During the early 1960s, an area informally called Larry's Lower Level, but more formally Axer's Alley, opened in the Gammage basement. The "Larry" was President J.

Opposite: The Gammage Building (1950s), built to accommodate a growing library, also housed administrative offices.

The 1957–1958 administration addition to the Gammage Building.

Lawrence Walkup, whose office was located directly above this student hall. Axer's Alley was a lounge and entertainment area with a dance floor and snack bar. It closed by the mid-1970s.

Biography

Grady Gammage was born on August 5, 1892, near Prescott, Arkansas. He lost his mother when he was quite young, leaving him to support himself. He graduated from high school in 1911 and taught in rural Arkansas schools for two years. He married Dixie Odile Dees of Amite, Iowa, in August 1913, and they soon moved west to Arizona, in part because Grady had contracted tuberculosis. He enrolled at the University of Arizona to study law, but switched academic programs and earned a bachelor's degree in education in 1916 and a master's degree in school administration in 1922.

Gammage became superintendent of the public schools for Winslow, Arizona, that same year and taught summer sessions in 1923, 1924, and 1925 at NANS. Upon accepting the position of vice president under President Fassett Cotton, Gammage moved permanently to Flagstaff in 1925. He became the seventh president of the institution in 1926. He received an honorary law degree from the University of Arizona (1927) and earned his doctorate from Columbia (1940).

Grady Gammage had an important and positive influence during his nearly eight-year tenure. He raised academic standards, cultivated a strong relationship between the campus and local community, and supported the first men's fraternity. He engaged in significant outreach to the local community, establishing a series of night classes for townspeople on subjects that included Spanish, business, and bookkeeping. He invited people from all over northern Arizona to visit the campus, believing that tours and discussions about the campus would generate support for the institution.

During his career at the school, Grady Gammage served as president of the American Society of Teachers Colleges. Later, he was a board member of the National War Fund and served as adviser to the Allied Military Government in Germany after World War II. He received the Legion of Merit from Denmark and a Certificate of Merit from China for these efforts. Grady Gammage left NASTC to become president of the state college in Tempe in 1933. He served in that role until his death on December 22, 1959, at age sixty-seven.

Grady Gammage, who served as president of both the Flagstaff and Tempe normal schools.

Gammage Building (2008). This portion of the building housed the college library. Note, in this photo, the lack of view of the administration addition, which is to the north, between the structure shown here and the Blome Building.

*The administration addition to the Gammage Building
(2008); Frier Hall is in the background.*

Open Forum House *(No Longer Standing)*

The Open Forum group on campus, formed prior to 1931, was dedicated to meaningful discussions on a wide range of topics. The group remained active, in various forms, until at least the 1960s. Weekly meetings, usually for one hour, were held on Sunday evenings, sometimes at faculty homes or in campus buildings such as Bury Hall and Gammage. Discussion topics included campus issues like the value of homecoming, national concerns such as the presidency of Franklin D. Roosevelt, and societal questions such as the role of women.

Plans developed for a separate structure for the Open Forum group during the fall of 1931. The plan was for a log-and-brick structure sixteen feet by twenty-four feet in size, to be shared for a time with the college YMCA group. Several campus events raised funds for the materials needed for the Open Forum House, which was designed in 1931 and constructed of plank and stone by students in 1932–1933. Among these events was the annual campus follies originated by Frank Brickey from Athletics and Physical Education—an annual tradition that continued long after the building was completed.

The Open Forum House was located a short distance southwest of the Riles Building and is visible on the 1946 aerial photograph. It was razed after 1949.

Open Forum House, completed by students in 1933, stood just southwest of the Riles Building.

North Hall

North Hall, constructed in 1931, was the final piece of the Women's Quadrangle. The structure is in the neoclassical style, symmetrical, and well balanced. There are flat pilasters on the front (north face) of the structure that resemble classical columns, and not a full portico. The exterior is of rectangular-style, rough-faced masonry with a Colonial Revival entrance. There is a Federal-style oval window above the entrance. The need for an additional student residence hall became evident at the start of school in 1931. Realizing the present facilities would be filled to capacity, the college made arrangements to have a thirty-two-room, wood-frame building constructed by a local firm, W. B. Goble. A group of businessmen put up the funding of $17,900 and the structure was completed in just one month; the businessmen recouped their investment through the rents paid by students. North Hall remains as a student residence hall and has the offices for Residence Life and the Office of Greek Life.

North Hall originally had a dining room and cafeteria in the basement. The dining facility, no longer needed for its original purpose, became a recreation area in 1950. Renovations occurred in 1954, 1958, 1985, and 2000. The 1954 renovations involved $350,000 the state legislature appropriated for a new education building. Deemed insufficient for the intended purpose, the funds provided renovations for Taylor Hall and North Hall. On those occasions each year when ABOR met in Flagstaff, they used the North Hall Lounge for their sessions until other suitable facilities, such as the University Union, became available. Today, North Hall and Morton Hall operate under a single name, North Morton Hall.

In the fall of 1949, the *Lumberjack* reported on a notorious resident of North Hall. Sniffles, a pet mouse, was held in great esteem by the ladies in the dorm, but the house mother disapproved and dispatched the mouse—thus snuffing out Sniffles. A week later, the *Lumberjack* ran a short follow-up story—a message from Sniffles living "on the other side" and enjoying all the cheese.

The north-facing entry to North Hall.

North Hall (2008).

64

Waggoner Fields

W. H. Waggoner, president of the Arizona Livestock Company and member of a prominent cattle-ranching family in Arizona, donated a twenty-eight-acre parcel of land to the college in 1937. Originally, this swath of land served portions of the college's agriculture curriculum. Waggoner Fields covered much of the area that is currently occupied by the Recreation Center, Lumberjack Stadium, the Wall Aquatic Center, corresponding parking lots, and part of the Mountain View Hall residence complex. Beginning in 1944 and continuing until the discontinuation of the sport at NAU in the early 1980s, the baseball diamond occupied a portion of Waggoner Fields. A football practice field and recreation fields filled in this landscape. The best view of Waggoner Fields is from aerial photographs of the campus.

Waggoner Fields, located on the eastern edge of campus, was named in honor of the donor, W. H. Waggoner. Numerous buildings occupy this land, including Lumberjack Stadium (visible in the center), the Recreation Center, Mountain View Hall, and the Wall Aquatic Center. The former President's House, later the Inn at NAU, is visible to the left. Mount Elden and downtown Flagstaff are in the background.

PRESIDENT LACEY EASTBURN AND THE TRANSITION TO ARIZONA STATE COLLEGE

In 1945, the governance of the three Arizona schools resided with a single Board of Regents. Arizona State Teachers College at Flagstaff became Arizona State College at Flagstaff. Open debate concerned the mission of the Flagstaff institution. The college at Tempe issued bachelor's degrees in arts and sciences, accompanying teacher training programs. Initially, ABOR declined to do the same for ASCF. Over the summer of 1946, ASCF obtained the right to grant bachelor's degrees in arts and sciences.

The conclusion of World War II brought surges in enrollment from veterans returning to civilian life. With more students and a change in overall mission, improvements for physical facilities were imperative. Plans called for a new physical education building, science facility, and athletic stadium. All of these occurred, though not immediately.

Lacey Eastburn helped avert a crisis early in his presidency. The North Central Association, which accredits schools, took a grim view of progress at ASCF. Concerns included an inadequate library and issues of workload, benefits, and retirement plans. The school needed a better mission statement and more rigorous grading. ASCF had less than a year to rectify these matters. Eastburn received funding for construction, for additional volumes for the library, and for recruiting faculty. Among the new faculty were J. Lawrence Walkup and Arthur Adel. Hanley Hall, remodeled, became a dormitory, the gymnasium was retrofitted to become the Women's Gymnasium, and a library addition and new heating plant with distribution tunnels throughout the campus were built. In late summer of 1951, sufficient improvements in the areas of concern resulted in a very positive response: full accreditation, including master's degree programs.

Physical plant changes during Eastburn's presidency (1947–1957) included the Atmospheric Research Observatory, a new science building (now Frier Hall), and a new student union. Lumberjack Gym opened in 1951 and the College Union, with its associated auditorium, was ready for use in early 1953.

By the mid-1950s, a remodel of Ashurst resulted in an excellent facility for music instruction and performances. Plans for what became the Eastburn Education Center included a new teacher training school. Skidmore Field, the old venue for athletics, became the site of two new dormitories—Peterson Hall and Babbitt Hall. Funds were approved for site work and relocation of the stadium (which became Lumberjack Stadium) to Waggoner Fields. Also approved was the addition of an administration wing to the Gammage Building.

From 1947 to 1957, faculty size increased from 47 to 67; student enrollment rose from 865 to 1,142; and $6 million was expended for new and renovated physical plant. All these developments set the course for sustained growth on the Flagstaff campus, which is the focus of chapter 3.

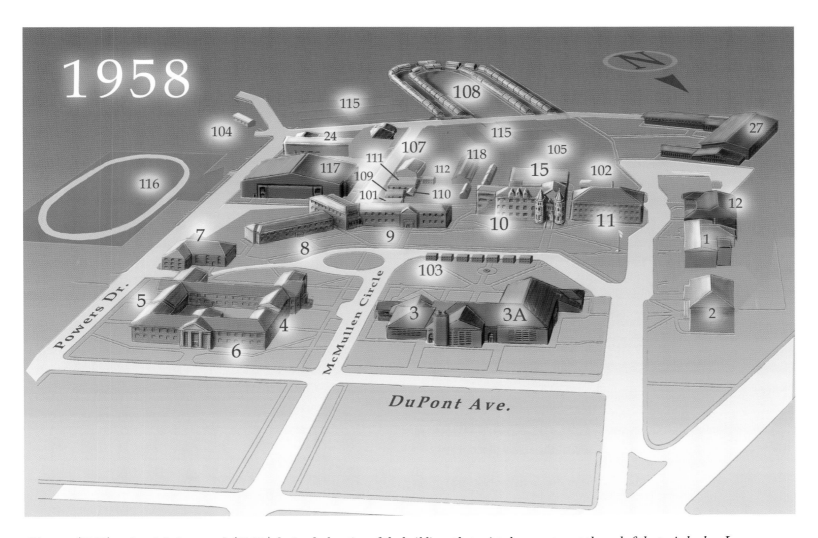

1958

The map (1958) and aerial photograph (1950s) depict the location of the buildings that existed on campus at the end of the period when Lacey Eastburn served as the college president. Though the photograph and map are not from exactly the same year, together they represent the campus as it appeared in about 1957, matching chapter 2 of the text and ending at the time the presidency of J. Lawrence Walkup began. Expansion southward began during the Eastburn years. Buildings that were new to this decade (1947–1957) are highlighted in orange on the map. (A key for building numbers is on page 301.)

Frier Hall

Frier Hall opened in the spring of 1950 as the Science Building. The name changed in 1961, honoring Della and Thomas Frier, who contributed $150,000 for scholarships. The Colonial Revival style is reminiscent of the capitol building at Colonial Williamsburg in Virginia. Symmetry is a key feature, with a central entrance and identical wings on either side. Interestingly, the patterned stonework on the front is very even, but not for the rear of the building. Frier Hall was the last campus building constructed using red Coconino sandstone. The metal roof is characteristic for buildings completed at the time.

When the new Science Building (currently home for Physics and Astronomy and Environmental Science) opened in 1964, all science departments, classes, and laboratories moved there from Frier Hall. Forestry and journalism programs relocated to Frier Hall. A complete interior renovation for the forestry program occurred in 1983–1985. During the renovations, Forestry moved temporarily to Old Main. U.S. Forest Service personnel occupied the structure just south of Frier Hall.

When the Southwest Forest Science Complex opened in 1992, the School of Forestry and the U.S. Forest Service moved to South Campus. The Department of Geology returned to Frier Hall and to the U.S. Forest Service Building, called the Geology Annex. Frier Hall houses classrooms and laboratories, research spaces, and offices for faculty, students, and staff in the Department of Geology. Here also are the Program for Quaternary Science and the Earthquake Information Center, which includes the Sherman Mifflin Smith Seismic Observatory, named for a geology student whose plane crashed in interior Alaska. In 1972, his parents provided funds to begin the Seismic Observatory. An array of sensors, distributed across northern Arizona, feed into a central location in Frier Hall, providing information on seismic activity for the southern Colorado Plateau.

Biographies

Della Carter Powell Frier was born in 1873 and arrived in Arizona with her parents in 1875. Thomas Conway Frier was born in Lampasas, Texas, in 1859 and moved to Arizona in 1884, where he worked on the Clay Park Ranch, thirty miles south of Flagstaff. Della and Thomas met in Flagstaff and married on August 18, 1895. Together, they owned a sizable cattle ranch near Lake Mary. Thomas was involved with both the state and national cattle growers associations. The Friers lived in what later became the J. R. Babbitt Sr. home near downtown Flagstaff. For 1917–1918, Della Frier was

Della and Thomas Frier.

Opposite: Frier Hall as the Science Building (early 1950s), with the name engraved above the entrance.

*The Forestry Department occupied Frier Hall from 1964
to 1992. Students and faculty are loading a field vehicle.*

Grand Matron for the Arizona chapter of the Eastern Star, a fraternal organization open to men and women whose purpose is to provide charitable, educational, and scientific support for worthy causes. By 1919, the Friers sold their ranching interests and moved to Phoenix. Mrs. Frier still summered in Flagstaff. Thomas Frier died on February 2, 1942, and Della Frier died on December 8, 1959, in Flagstaff. Mrs. Frier's will provided that part of her estate, in the form of $150,000 of stock in the AT&T Company, go to the state college in Flagstaff to support scholarships. Though neither of the Friers had a direct connection to the college, they nevertheless believed in its mission and supported its future.

Frier Hall (2008) is home to the Department of Geology.

*In 1967, the U.S. Forest Service constructed a research laboratory
adjacent to Frier Hall, visible in the background.*

Geology Annex

This structure, built with federal money in 1967, housed
the research component of the Forest Service for this
region. Previously, the Rocky Mountain Forest Experi-
ment Station was located in the Blome Building. The
structure represents an early modern version of the
International style, with Roman bricks, spandrel panels,
and the characteristic metal mullions that surround
the plate-glass windows. The north entrance is in a
Craftsman-like style, reflecting a waning connection to
pre–World War II Bungalow building traditions. When
the Southwest Forest Science Complex opened in 1992,
the Forest Service operations moved to South Campus
and the Department of Geology moved from the Science
Building to both Frier Hall and the U.S. Forest Service
Building (Geology Annex). The Annex has faculty offices,
research laboratories, and a seminar room.

When the Forest Service moved to South Campus, its research lab became the Geology Annex.

Skidmore Field *(No Longer Present)*

Skidmore Field was dedicated on October 28, 1933, and replaced McMullen Field as the primary outdoor athletic grounds. It occupied the site that is the home of the Science Building, the Liberal Arts Building, and portions of Peterson and Babbitt Halls. The northern border was Ellery Street, and Lumberjack Gym was later located behind the bleachers on the west side of the field. Wooden bleachers were installed at Skidmore Field in 1933 and a cinder track soon thereafter. Stadium seating replaced the wooden bleachers for the fall 1948 season and lights provided illumination for evening practices and games. The lights were a gift from the Flagstaff Chamber of Commerce. The first night event was a football game on September 18, 1948. The stadium seating moved from Skidmore Field to what became Lumberjack Stadium. As the campus expanded, Lumberjack Stadium replaced Skidmore Field—the last game at Skidmore Field was played in 1956.

Biography

William Ralph Skidmore died on December 6, 1932, at just thirty-seven years of age, after suffering a cerebral hemorrhage while duck hunting at Lake Mary in late November. He was born on July 20, 1895, in Curtin, Oregon, spent his early years there, and graduated from the nearby Cottage Grove High School.

He was a veteran of World War I, serving with the U.S. Army Corps of Engineers. Skidmore received his bachelor's (1920) and master's (1922) degrees from the University of Oregon and his doctorate, in physics, from the University of Iowa (1925). He came to Flagstaff in 1929 after four years as a member of the faculty at Ottawa University in Kansas.

During his brief sojourn in Flagstaff, he was a member of the American Legion, the College Science Club, and the Methodist Episcopal Church. A physicist by training, Skidmore served as head of the Science Department on campus and as the first president of the new Border Athletic Conference from 1931 to 1932. He was a very popular and gifted teacher. He was a member of the Honor Lodge of the American Chemical Society and four honorary professional fraternities, attesting to his great success, even at a relatively young age.

William Skidmore was a member of the science faculty and served as the first president of the new Border Athletic Conference from 1931 to 1932.

*Skidmore Field, with associated bleacher seating, replaced
McMullen Field as the location for outdoor athletics.*

Heating Plant/Plateau Center

A new heating and physical plant debuted in 1949. Electrical power was available from public sources, so only the heating function was necessary. Construction of this facility included heating tunnels, forming a distribution system throughout campus. The structure is modern in architectural style with no particularly noteworthy attributes, representing the nonstylistic beginnings of the postwar modern era. Beginning almost immediately, there were modifications, additions, and equipment replacement. Garages, storage buildings, and maintenance sheds that were located in the area disappeared over time but were key parts of the physical plant functions for the entire campus. At times, portions of the physical plant and maintenance operations inhabited the basements of Taylor and Bury Halls. The campus linen service had its final home in the Plateau Center, before discontinuance in the mid-1990s.

The building's name has changed from Physical Plant to Physical Resources to, in 1989, Heating Plant, and then to Plateau Center in 1992. This structure was sometimes referred to as the North Heating Plant. By the mid-1960s, almost all aspects of physical plant operations and maintenance for the campus were clustered in this structure and the associated buildings.

In 1980, a major renovation ($480,000) began a shift to other uses for the building and diminution of physical plant operations at this location, though some functions remain today, such as boilers serving portions of North Campus. Plans to move some of these functions to the Coconino County Yard were shelved when construction of a new facility for physical plant operations superseded this move. During recent years, the Colorado Plateau Research Station of the U.S. Geological Survey occupied portions of the building. Other current or recent tenants include the refrigerator concession of the Association of University Residence Halls (AURH), a laundry operation, offices, a machine shop, and the Sculpture Studio.

During the course of the 1980s and 1990s, the university expended $530,000 for upgrades, remodeling, and meeting building code specifications. A new boiler went into operation in early 1984 to augment the three existing boilers. In the summer of 2006, the Sculpture Studio migrated from the Heating Plant Building to the former Recycling Building on South Campus. Due to safety concerns and other hazards, a portion of the Plateau Center is no longer habitable; decisions about its future are under discussion.

The Heating Plant (early 1950s) was modified several times over the years.

The Heating Plant Building was renamed the Plateau Center (2008).

Storage Buildings, Warehouses, Shops, Greenhouse, and Garages

An operation as large as the institution at Flagstaff requires space for servicing equipment, garaging vehicles, general storage, doing laundry, and myriad operational functions. During the almost 110 years of the campus, many such structures appeared and disappeared from maps and written records. Structures served more than one purpose or changed functions over time. Most of the buildings referred to here belong with the physical plant operations (Capital Assets and Services). Some maintenance and storage structures are visible on maps and aerial photographs reproduced in this book.

A sequence of buildings shown south of Taylor Hall on several of the early campus maps involved different structures and functions over time. Two were simple cottages; one cottage served as the Home Management House, and both housed students at various times. The structure immediately south of Taylor Hall was the original heating and power plant. For a period, one structure served as the college infirmary. During the period shortly after World War II and into the early 1950s, a Quonset hut served as a classroom building. Another building, moved to the campus as part of the federal assistance program, was a large metalworking shop, the Machine Metal Shop, located not far from where the Plateau Center is today.

The southernmost building on the 1949 campus map was a greenhouse. Authorized in 1939 and built at a cost of $3,000 by the National Greenhouse Co. of Pana, Illinois, the glass-enclosed structure and attached workhouse served primarily as a place to produce plants and flowers for campus landscaping. Today there is a research Greenhouse Complex at the south end of campus and a teaching greenhouse associated with biology.

At the south end of this group was a bus barn. During the 1930s through the 1960s, ASCF used a series of beloved buses to transport students to athletic contests and other school functions. Students bestowed monikers on these vehicles, such as "Yellow Fever," "Travel Jack," and "Blue Boy."

Opposite: The Machine Metal Shop (late 1940s) was located to the south of Taylor Hall.

Lumberjack Gymnasium

(No Longer Standing)

With the growth of athletics before and after World War II, new facilities were required. The Physical Education Building, soon named Lumberjack Gym, was dedicated on February 7, 1951. The outer walls were of red sandstone, accented with copper. At the first event in the new men's gym, the basketball Lumberjacks defeated Hardin-Simmons, 66–56. Previously, men's basketball games were contested in the gymnasium at Flagstaff High School or the Riles Building. Plans called for a structure that was twice the size of the eventual structure. Lumberjack Gym had an indoor track in a "U" shape with start and finish lines at opposite ends of the same wall. A completed gymnasium track would have been a traditional full oval. The seating capacity had foldaway seating for 1,000 people on each side and 1,300 other seats at floor level, for a total capacity of 3,300.

When the internationally renowned pianist Van Cliburn came to campus, he was scheduled to play at Lumberjack Gym. His piano recital was to begin at 8 p.m., but there was a major snowstorm in progress. The starting time passed with no sign of the guest performer. Instead of driving to the concert, Van Cliburn decided to walk from the Holiday Inn, located on Milton Road, to the concert venue. He got lost, arrived an hour late, and gave a superb performance.

As the college evolved into a university, a series of venues hosted public performances and concerts. The assembly hall in Old Main was replaced by the auditorium in Ashurst. However, bigger venues were required and Lumberjack Gym filled this need from 1951 to 1989. Among those who performed at the gym were the Fifth Dimension, Al Hirt, Gladys Knight and the Pips, Ray Charles, the Nitty Gritty Dirt Band, John Denver, Gordon Lightfoot, and Buddy Rich. The gym served as a location for commencements for many years.

A flu epidemic on campus in 1956 overwhelmed the infirmary, and Lumberjack Gym served as temporary quarters for sick students. In 1973, attempts to control a termite infestation led to a serious warping of the gym floor, from water used in the eradication process. A complete resurfacing was necessary.

An addition in 1972 provided space for offices, classrooms, locker rooms, and Athletics. The building was home to the college's basketball teams for twenty-six years, which then moved to the Skydome starting in 1977. For some years thereafter, Athletics retained office space in the gym, though many coaches and staff moved first to Lumberjack Stadium and later to the Skydome. The old gym had several classrooms and offices for humanities faculty for a time. As safety issues mounted and the need to undertake expensive repairs increased, Lumberjack Gym was condemned. Lahaina Construction carried out demolition in 1997 at a cost of $300,000.

Lumberjack Gymnasium (1960s).

North Union and Prochnow Auditorium (College Union)

Beginning in 1938, discussion began concerning a central gathering place for students. The Dairy Barn, abandoned in 1940 when the school sold its herd of cattle, was a possible union building, but events of World War II intervened and the structure was too distant from Central Campus. After the war, a group lobbied for a building that would be a memorial to those from the college who served in the military and for the faculty who served the institution. In addition, many alumni gatherings and other events happened off campus because no suitable venue existed on campus.

In the fall of 1946, ABOR approved a design for a student union consisting of a central building with two wings, constructed as a log structure. By 1949–1950, plans had moved forward and a site, located north of Old Main and the fountain, was chosen. Part of this land was in use as the playground for the Training School students. The 1951–1952 session of the state legislature approved funds for construction of a building that would include an auditorium and a dining hall. The North Union, Dining Hall, and Prochnow Auditorium were built as a single structure. The North Union served a variety of student needs with lounge areas, the bookstore, and space for student groups. The Dining Hall provided a much-needed addition for student meals. Prochnow Auditorium became a major venue for university events.

The building, opened in 1952, exhibits the International modern style with lots of plate glass and little ornamentation, though some Colonial Revival features indicate this as a transitional building into the postwar modern era of architecture that swept the nation up until the 1980s. The college bookstore was located in this building (1953–1967)

and then moved to its present location on Central Campus. There were three apartments in the North Union, the largest of which had two bedrooms; these were used to house visiting scholars. Joe Rolle and his family lived here during the time he managed the bookstore. Over its first half century the structure contained a number of units, such as Food Services, Student Services, organizations involved with student government including the Associated Students of Northern Arizona University (ASNAU), the offices of the Dean of Students and Student Life, the International and Study Abroad Programs, and the Association of University Residence Halls. Occupants of the North Union today include the Timberline Inn (with food service) and University Marketing. Recently, New Student Programs and Student Orientation moved from the North Union to renovated quarters in Sechrist Hall.

Prochnow Auditorium is home to a number of social events, performances, university and academic ceremonies, speeches from prominent visitors, and conferences. It has a seating capacity of 950. Prochnow Auditorium, originally called College Auditorium and later University Auditorium, was named to honor Robert Prochnow in the fall of 1985. The new auditorium supplanted Ashurst as the location for most cultural performances and speakers. Among those who performed at Prochnow Auditorium were the Kingston Trio; Dave Brubeck; Dionne Warwick; Peter, Paul, and Mary; Lucille Ball; the Smothers Brothers; and the Broadway cast of the musical *Jesus Christ Superstar*. Speakers at this venue included George Plimpton, William Sloane Coffin, Howard K. Smith, Paul Ehrlich, Dick Gregory, Billy Mills, and Sherman Alexie.

Front of the North Union and Prochnow Auditorium (1950s)
soon after it opened, with "ASC" lettering on the chimney.

North Union in winter, with "NAU" lettering on the chimney.

Biography

Robert W. Prochnow was a member of the Arizona State Legislature for ten years and a strong advocate for Flagstaff and the college. He was born on November 16, 1909, in Flagstaff, the oldest of twelve children of a pioneer family. His father worked in the lumber mills and met his mother in Flagstaff. Prochnow attended St. Anthony's Academy, Flagstaff High School, and Arizona State Teachers College at Flagstaff. He also attended the University of Arizona for a time. As a young man, he worked in lumber mills, operating machinery that made fruit and vegetable boxes. He worked as a bellhop at the Commercial Hotel, an establishment owned by his father. He was a clerk and then an accountant and credit manager for the Babbitt Brothers Trading Company. During the Great Depression, Prochnow's employment was subject to the vicissitudes of the economic climate. He briefly managed a service station, moved to California where times were equally difficult, and returned to Flagstaff where he ran the Arrowhead Motel, now the Twilight Motel, on Route 66.

Prochnow served in the Navy Seabees during World War II. When he returned to Flagstaff, he operated a cigar store and newsstand. He was a founder of the American Legion post established after World War II and later served (1945–1946) as state commander of the American Legion. He chaired the local March of Dimes for twenty-five years,

at a time when polio was prominent and efforts to eradicate the disease increased.

Prochnow was first elected to the state senate in 1952. He chaired the Senate Appropriations Committee for much of his time in the legislature. One of Prochnow's most significant accomplishments was securing funding for a new School of Forestry at Flagstaff. Training in forest science began in 1939 and involved summer school classes. Prochnow played a prominent role in establishing the School of Nursing as well. He was involved with creating the junior (community) college system in Arizona. He followed his service in the state legislature with eight years as a member of the Coconino County Board of Supervisors. After retirement in 1973, Prochnow moved to Montezuma, Arizona, and died there in 1986.

Robert W. Prochnow, Flagstaff native and state senator.

Front view of the North Union and Prochnow Auditorium (2007).

Atmospheric Research Observatory

The Atmospheric Research Observatory opened in 1953. Prior to that date, considerable astronomical research took place in the Flagstaff area. Lowell Observatory drew attention to Flagstaff's clear night skies and excellent atmospheric conditions. President Thomas Tormey partnered with Cornell University to establish an astronomical observatory on campus in 1938. The earlier facility, termed "Cornell in Arizona," featured what was then the largest telescope (24 inches) in the world. Dr. R. W. Shaw from Cornell University led the effort, with the primary purpose of studying meteors. The telescope was housed in a shelter built on the site of the present observatory. Cornell scientists, scholars from Lowell Observatory, and local faculty and students shared the use of this facility. Cooperation between the college and Lowell Observatory continues today, with considerable reciprocal benefits to NAU students and faculty as well as the scholarly community at Lowell.

A special ABOR meeting, held in June 1950, approved plans for a new, more permanent observatory. The U.S. government provided an allowance of $120,000 for construction and related telescopic equipment. The key individual involved in obtaining funds for the new Atmospheric Research Observatory was Dr. Arthur Adel, the namesake of the building that currently houses the Department of Mathematics and Statistics. Adel was a prominent astronomer and physicist, using the observatory as part of his efforts to discover and elucidate planetary atmospheric characteristics, specifically with infrared spectroscopy.

The Atmospheric Research Laboratory has two pylons used to roll out moving roofs, exposing telescopes. The facility houses a primary 24-inch reflecting telescope and six 10-inch telescopes. Although the use of the facility for serious atmospheric research has passed, the university uses it for classes in astronomy and public programs. In 2008, plans were in place for the addition of a new 20-inch Ritchey-Chrétien telescope, provided for by a donation from Professors Barry Lutz and Susanna Maxwell. Atmospheric and astronomical investigations, particularly with student classes, have used the roofs of several science buildings for their observations.

A view of the Atmospheric Research Observatory (ca. 1955).

*The Atmospheric Research Observatory (2007), looking
south, with rollout structures for moving telescopes.*

Eastburn Education Center

The need for a new structure to house the education departments was evident in 1948 when the budget from the state included funds for a new Training School. An appropriation of $200,000 by the state legislature in 1955 was insufficient for construction of the building, so, in 1956, the legislature appropriated an additional $1 million to complete the job. Construction of the Eastburn Education Center began in 1957, during the last year of Lacey Eastburn's tenure as president of ASCF. The building opened in December 1958, was dedicated on March 10, 1959, and housed the departments that comprised the College of Education and the Training School. The first floor of the main building contained a library for students, faculty, and teachers, faculty offices, and several lounges. Classes and seminars were held on the second floor. The Training School, located in the southern wing of the building, featured classrooms and a gymnasium. The Eastburn Education Center is a good example of modern or International style of architecture, which dominated civic and commercial buildings through the 1980s. A key feature of this period is the pattern of the metal mullions that separate the plate-glass windows.

The Training School eventually closed in 1983. Initially, grades 4–6 were eliminated in stages, beginning in 1980, and the remaining 102 students in kindergarten and grades 1–3 were transferred to other schools over the next three years. During much of its existence, the student population consisted of children of faculty and children from families living in the South Side neighborhood. The Training School served as the Eastburn Education and Research Center, referring to faculty efforts to design and implement new pedagogies, using the Training School classes as a testing ground.

The Training School portion of the building was renovated shortly after it closed and served first as a backstage area for the Theatre Department, which was later relocated to the Performing Arts Building. Eventually, the Training School gymnasium was converted to a curriculum library. The old gymnasium now has a false ceiling. In 1996, a renovation of the second floor reconfigured the space, provided changes to meet new building codes, and added space for new learning technologies. From 1985 to June 2002, the College of Education bore the name Center for Excellence in Education. In the early 1970s, Educational Psychology split from the Department of Psychology and formed a separate unit that was primarily devoted to clinical psychology and educational psychology.

Two other structures are closely associated with the College of Education and some of its broader functions: the Institute for Human Development and the Education Annex.

Today, the Eastburn Education Center houses the offices of the College of Education, of the four main departments that comprise the college, of faculty, and of graduate students; classrooms; and several teacher resource centers. The departments are Educational Leadership, Teaching and Learning, Educational Specialties, and Educational Psychology. Portions of the faculty and some of the programs associated with the College of Education found homes in the Riles Building and the Educational Annex at different times.

Eastburn Education Center, with the Training School on the left and main entrance to the right.

Eastburn Education Center (2007).

Biography

Lacey Arnold Eastburn was born on May 19, 1889, in South English, Iowa. His family moved to rural Missouri when he was a young man. He attended school five months a year, completed the eighth grade at age nineteen, and success-fully passed the teacher certification test. Prior to obtaining his bachelor's degree, Eastburn taught in rural Missouri public schools for four years. He received his bachelor of science in education at Southwest Missouri State Teachers College (Missouri State University) at Springfield in 1916 with three years of concerted effort. He earned a master's degree from Drury College in the same city in 1917.

Shortly after completing service as a lieutenant in the Army Air Corps during World War I, he joined the Northern Arizona Normal School faculty in 1919 as an instructor in mathematics and physics and supervisor of practice teaching. His wife, Viola, also joined the NANS faculty in the Education Department. Two years later, they moved to Phoenix where Lacey served on the faculty at Phoenix Junior College. Eastburn studied at the University of Arizona and the University of California at Berkeley, and obtained a doctorate from Stanford University in 1947.

Upon completing his doctorate, Eastburn returned to Flagstaff as president of Arizona State College, a posi-tion he held for ten years. During his tenure, he led a successful campaign to prevent the North Central Asso-ciation from removing ASC's accreditation. Eastburn addressed weaknesses noted by the accrediting body. His response to the accreditation crisis is detailed in the introduction to this chapter.

A second major achievement of Eastburn's presidency was managing the increase in enrollment from returning World War II veterans. He devised creative provisions to accommodate the influx of students, who needed both living quarters and classrooms. Last, Eastburn set in motion a series of building projects on campus, including Frier Hall (for sciences), the Atmospheric Research Observatory, the North Union and Prochnow Auditorium, several residence halls, and the education building that bears his name.

Lacey Eastburn died on October 31, 1957, in Cotton-wood, Arizona, where he had gone for a month's leave of absence due to illness. He is the only sitting president of what is now Northern Arizona University to die in office. Dean J. Lawrence Walkup succeeded him, first on an interim basis and then permanently, beginning in Decem-ber 1957.

Lacey Eastburn, the tenth president of Arizona State College.

Institute for Human Development

Growing out of the programs in the College of Education, the Institute for Human Development opened in 1966 as an addition to the southwest section of the Eastburn Education Center. Many of the programs housed in the institute benefit citizens of Arizona, particularly northern Arizona. The building contains offices, meeting rooms, and several laboratories. Many of the staff and most of the programs in the Institute for Human Development receive funding through grants and contracts. Consistent with the time, the structure is in the modern International style, similar to the Eastburn Education Center. An Arizona Rehabilitation Services grant provided a significant portion of the building's cost.

Among the groups housed in the Institute for Human Development are programs pertaining to behavioral issues, early intervention projects, and Native Americans, as well as initiatives involving technology resources and services, rehabilitation services, and aspects of special education. Members of the institute's staff were early proponents of teaching Spanish as a second language as well as promoting education for the visually handicapped. Several graduate certificates are awarded in disability policy and practice and positive behavior support. The NAU Office of Disability Support Services, now Disability Resources, was located in the Institute for Human Development for many years, before moving to the Ponderosa Building.

The Institute for Human Development was added to the Eastburn Education Center in 1966 to house a series of programs relating to education, rehabilitation, and special services that serve northern Arizona.

Education Annex

This prefabricated building is located at the north end of the parking lot separating Babbitt Academic Annex and Peterson Hall. The university purchased the building and moved it to this site in 1996. For several years, the structure was home to programs from the College of Education.

At the beginning of the twenty-first century the building housed, for a time, the offices of Distance Learning. In summer 2007 the structure "reopened" to house the Laboratory of Quaternary Paleontology.

The Education Annex is a prefabricated structure purchased in 1996 and situated just east of Babbitt Academic Annex.

THE WALKUP ERA AND BECOMING NORTHERN ARIZONA UNIVERSITY

Significant changes to the college physical plant occurred during the twenty-two years that J. Lawrence Walkup was president. Walkup came to NAU in 1949 and rapidly assumed a succession of administrative roles. When Lacey Eastburn fell ill and left the college for a month's leave of absence in October 1957, Walkup became interim president. Sadly, Eastburn passed away later in the month; Walkup was formally appointed president in December 1957.

During the years that Walkup was president, the college became Northern Arizona University, and more than fifty buildings were added to the institution, including an entire new campus, the South Academic Center. Staggering growth of the university, from 1,098 to 11,601 students and a faculty that increased from 107 to 651, occurred during this time. As Walkup became president, the college exceeded its capacity to house students on campus and local motels were leased for overflow. It was during this era that students began to live off campus.

The first two buildings completed during Walkup's tenure were Peterson and Babbitt Halls, both dormitories. Two student residences, Gillenwater Hall (called South Quadrangle) and Stroud Hall (Roseberry), opened in the ensuing two years. What students viewed as "South Campus" kept moving farther south. This process began with cottages in 1939–1940 and marched onward with construction of student residence halls (McDonald, Cowden, Tinsley, and Raymond) by the mid-1960s. To support the

increased enrollment, new dining facilities were required. A new President's House was built southeast of the campus and, west of that, a Home Management House.

The Walkup years brought changes in the academic structure at the college, beginning with a reorganization of academic units into seven divisions: Teacher Education, Business Administration and Economics, Forestry, Science and Mathematics, Liberal Arts, Technology and Applied Arts, and General Studies. New academic buildings included the Applied Arts and Technology Building (School of Communications), a Science Building (the first structure of today's Science Complex), and the Liberal Arts Building.

By the mid-1960s, other buildings were added to Central Campus. These included dormitories (Wilson, Sechrist, Allen, and Reilly) and Campus Heights Apartments, a dining facility called University Commons, a new library, a bookstore, and a student health center. The University Union Field House and Lumberjack Stadium enhanced athletics and recreation.

In the latter half of the 1960s, new academic structures appeared, including Biology and Chemistry Buildings; the Performing and Fine Arts Building, soon joined by Ardrey Auditorium; and research facilities in the form of the Institute for Human Development and the Geology Annex. When the institution became Northern Arizona University in 1966, a reorganization created five colleges (Arts and Sciences, Business Administration, Creative Arts, Education,

and Graduate Studies) and two schools (Forestry and Applied Sciences and Technology).

In October 1966, a plan was announced to have three campuses at NAU. Two of these, the current North Campus and South Campus, were designated as North and South Academic Centers. The third campus, never built, was to emphasize engineering. Construction of fifteen buildings at the South Academic Center included academic buildings, a large dormitory, a dining facility, an activity center, a small library, and an administration building.

During the 1970s, a plan for establishing an American Indian School of Medicine at NAU was discussed, but lacked sufficient support. In the late 1970s, the university built and maintained an electronic message board for several years. Located along Milton Road, behind Gammage, it provided information about events at NAU and publicity for the school. Fittingly, one of the last two buildings constructed at NAU during the Walkup presidency is named in his honor: the J. Lawrence Walkup Skydome.

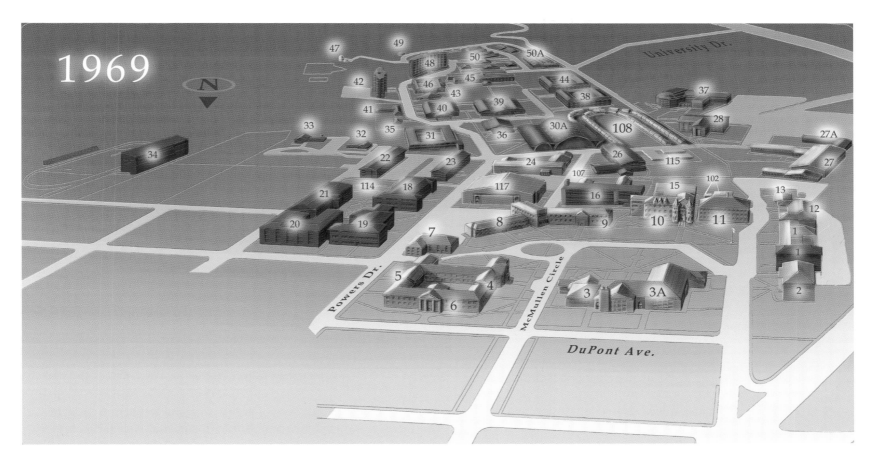

1969

The map and aerial photograph (both 1969) depict the location of the buildings that existed on campus at the midpoint of the presidency of J. Lawrence Walkup. All buildings highlighted in orange were constructed during the first twelve years of the Walkup presidency. Much of this growth involved filling in portions of the North Campus and Central Campus. These changes match the first half of the text of chapter 3. (A key for building numbers is on page 301.)

Peterson Hall

Peterson Hall was constructed as part of a pair of student residence halls, the other being Babbitt Hall. Opened in 1958 and dedicated on April 8, 1959, Peterson Hall is representative of the International-style postwar modern architecture that dominated in America and Europe from the 1950s to the 1980s. Its design is purely functional, boxlike with ribbon windows. For much of its existence, the structure served as a men's residence. The three-story building contains 84 rooms and housed up to 158 students.

An amusing anecdote involves the resident family, a barnyard animal, and mischievous students. The family, the Schneblys, unknowingly hosted a sheep for an evening. Just before the winter holidays, a local church had a manger scene that included live sheep. Enterprising students captured one sheep and tethered it to the door of the Schneblys' apartment. By the next morning there was quite an organic redolence emanating from newly deposited egesta in the hall. The students paid the bill for a complete holiday dinner for the custodian who cleaned up after the sheep.

Approximately $250,000 was spent during the first years of the new millennium for repairs and recovery after a major flood, as well as transforming the dormitory to office space. In 2004, the building became swing space, occupied by different offices and programs as renovations and new construction occurred at various locations on campus. Units relocated to Peterson for varying periods or on a semipermanent basis include Faculty Development Program, Assessment, Grants and Contract services, the Merriam-Powell Center for Environmental Research, the Native American Cancer Research Partnership, and faculty from departments and programs such as Engineering and Exercise Science.

Biography

Andrew Christian Peterson was born on September 24, 1870, in Gunnison, Utah. He graduated from high school at Brigham Young University in 1896, obtaining his bachelor's degree from the same school in 1916, and later a master's degree from the University of Utah.

He served as a member of the Graham County Board of Supervisors and was a member of the State Constitutional Convention. Peterson served as principal of schools for St. Johns, Eager, and Gila Academy in Thatcher, and as a school superintendent in Spanish Fork, Utah. He was elected to the Arizona State Legislature and served as Speaker of the House in the 4th Session for 1919–1920. He was State Superintendent of Instruction for Arizona in 1920.

A. C. Peterson joined the faculty at Northern Arizona State Teachers College in 1927 and served until 1944, by which time the institution's name had changed to Arizona State Teachers College at Flagstaff. He taught courses in political science and education. In 1940, he became an honorary member of the University of Arizona Law School Students Association.

Andrew C. Peterson.

The entry of Peterson Hall dormitory (1959).

In 1937, Peterson, a member of the Church of Jesus Christ of Latter-Day Saints, announced plans for a joint venture between the college and the church headquarters in Salt Lake City. This resulted in an institute building, constructed east of Campbell Hall. This structure, next to the College Inn on Powers Street, was at a location occupied currently by the Wettaw Building.

Peterson was the commencement speaker at Arizona State College in spring 1946. He also spoke that year at the dedication of a new organ for the college, donated in honor of his son, Arman Peterson, killed in World War II when his plane was shot down over France. Arman was a past president of the student body at the college. Andrew Peterson died on July 27, 1955, in Phoenix.

Peterson Hall entryway (2008).

West side of Peterson Hall (2008).

Babbitt Hall/
Babbitt Academic Annex

Babbitt Hall, named in honor of James E. Babbitt Sr., opened at the same time as Peterson Hall. Originally it was referred to as Dormitory #1 and then as Dorm B. The architecture, characterized as typical of the International modern style, is nearly identical to Peterson's style. The design is purely functional, with the same boxlike appearance and ribbon windows. A significant remodel in 1990 converted the building from a dormitory to offices for academic departments. Babbitt Academic Annex houses the Departments of Philosophy and Modern Languages, and some faculty from the English Department. There are a language laboratory, seminar rooms, and several classrooms in addition to the faculty and departmental offices.

Biography

James E. Babbitt Sr. was born on September 28, 1902, in Santa Monica, California. After beginning his training at the School of Law of Loyola University (California), he received his law degree from the University of Southern California. Babbitt then earned a master of science degree from Georgetown University in Washington, D.C. After briefly practicing law in Los Angeles, he became the corporate lawyer for the Babbitt Brothers Trading Company in 1929.

His first election to the Arizona State Legislature in 1933 made him the youngest member of that body. Among his legislative accomplishments was assisting with the bill that gave ASTCF the right to grant master's degrees in education. He was reelected for a second term in the Arizona State House and then, for successive terms until his death in 1944, to the Arizona State Senate. In the latter body, he was chair of the Appropriations Committee for three terms. He was a strong supporter of the college at Flagstaff, the city, and northern Arizona. Babbitt played key roles in securing a minimum wage for public works projects, the old age pension bill, the Power Authority Act, and game and fish legislation.

Babbitt served on the executive committee for the Boy Scouts and as a member of the Rotary, Elks, and Knights of Columbus. He held leadership positions in several of these organizations. Always interested in culture and the arts, he provided support for both the Flagstaff Community Players and local community concerts. He served as a board member for the Arizona Wool Growers Association and as president of the Arizona Game Protection Association.

On November 7, 1944, he went bear hunting east of Camp Verde, near Fossil Creek and Strawberry. He was recovering from a bout of influenza at the time. When a storm bringing rain and snow caught the group unprepared, he became separated from his companions; his body was found on November 13. He had been elected to another term in the state legislature just days before his death. His brother, John Babbitt, was appointed to take his place. His promising political career, which may have included the office of governor, ended and Arizona lost a valued citizen.

James E. Babbitt Sr.

Babbitt Hall (1960s). Peterson and Babbitt Halls were built at the same time and are virtually identical on the exterior, though their entrances are somewhat different.

View of Babbitt Academic Annex looking northeast (2008).

Stroud Hall/ Roseberry Apartments

In June 1959, ABOR approved the concept for what would become Stroud Hall. L. L. Stroud, a local businessman, constructed a motel off Route 66 (Milton Road), associated with the nearby Park Plaza Motel, which he owned. A three-year lease with ABOR provided housing for 150 female students during the academic year (thirty-eight weeks), and the structure reverted to a motel during the fourteen-week summer tourist season. The motel/dormitory opened in 1962 with the top two floors housing women who were part of sororities (Delta Delta Delta and Gamma Phi Beta) and the lower floor serving for independent women students. For at least one year, 1968–1969, Stroud Hall was home to one fraternity, and a hair salon occupied a second-floor room during a period when it was Stroud Hall. The building has motel-style features and is typical of 1960s roadside architecture.

Local businessman George Nackard purchased Stroud Hall and sold it to the state for $1.05 million in the late 1960s. Renamed in honor of Minnie Roseberry, it served as a dormitory for women and men at various times. After renovations in 1984, it became residential apartments, and today it contains fifty-two studio apartments for married couples without children and for women students.

Biography

Minnie Roseberry was born in 1896 in Kansas, received her bachelor of arts from Kansas State Teachers College (Emporia State University) in 1925, and earned a master's degree from Teachers College at Columbia University in 1931. That same year, she moved to Flagstaff to join the Training School staff at NASTC. She taught kindergarten and first grade for more than three decades with the college Training School and was the instructor for numerous classes in the teacher training curriculum. She obtained her doctorate in education from the University of Maryland in 1958.

During World War II, Roseberry went through the Red Cross nurse's aide program and served more than a thousand hours as a volunteer, working on weekends and during school holidays and for two summers. She served as the northern Arizona representative for the White House Conference on Children and Youth in 1950. Over the course of her career, Roseberry received several honors, including Woman of the Day (1961), a Distinguished Faculty Award (1964), and Flagstaff Citizen of the Year (1969). She retired in 1967 and died in October 1982.

Minnie Roseberry.

Stroud Hall (1962), when it served as a student dormitory. During summer months, this building was a motel, located just off Route 66 (now Milton Road).

Roseberry Apartments (2008).

South Quadrangle/
Gillenwater Hall

South Quadrangle opened in 1958 and was dedicated on November 9 of that year. It contained a series of modest apartments for married students. The original design called for forty-eight apartments but grew to sixty-seven during construction. The name changed in 1987 to honor Virgil Gillenwater. Its architectural style is late International, similar to structures built as motels or apartments along U.S. roadsides in the 1950s and 1960s. Obvious features are the overall boxy design, latticework, and ribbon windows.

Initially, South Quadrangle housed women during the academic year and was set aside for students with families during summer sessions of the 1960s. In the mid-1980s, the rock face on the north side of the building was used for rock-climbing instruction. Today, Gillenwater Hall houses both men and women in its apartment-style living quarters. Three students share each apartment and both nine- and twelve-month leases accommodate different student needs. The central courtyard is a gathering place and focus of many activities for those living in Gillenwater Hall.

Biography

Virgil Gillenwater was born on February 26, 1915, in Sciota, Illinois, and graduated from high school in nearby Rushville in 1934. He obtained his bachelor of arts from Western Illinois State Teachers College (Western Illinois University), followed by master of science and doctorate degrees from the University of Illinois. He served for five years as an infantryman in the U.S. Army.

With the exception of an eighteen-month break when he was president of Trenton State College (Trenton State University) in New Jersey, Gillenwater served the college for almost thirty years, arriving in 1950 and retiring in 1980. He began as director of Student Teaching and then became head of the Education Department. He was director of Student Placement and, when Lawrence Walkup became president, Gillenwater was appointed as executive dean. He became executive vice president when university status was granted to the college in 1966.

Gillenwater was a member of the National Council on Accreditation of Teacher Education and chair of the State Advisory Commission of Teacher Certification. He was a founding member of the NAU chapter of the honor society Phi Kappa Phi. He was the homecoming dedicatee in 1971 and received an honorary doctor of letters degree in 1978. Throughout his career, Gillenwater actively supported the local community and was a key bridge between the college and the city. He died on March 31, 1986, in Sedona. The Virgil and Clarine Gillenwater Scholarship Fund provides financial aid to needy students at NAU.

Virgil Gillenwater.

Left: South Quadrangle (1960) soon after it opened.

Below: Gillenwater Hall (2008).

Constructed at different times and for different purposes, three structures comprise today's School of Hotel and Restaurant Management (HRM). They appear in the following three entries in chronological order.

President's House/ The Inn at NAU

When Lawrence and Lucy Walkup arrived in Flagstaff in the late 1940s, they resided in the Clark Homes, just west of downtown. These accommodations had several problems, one of which was a hole in the floor where the previous occupants had chopped wood for the stove. President Lacey Eastburn had the garage of his home converted as a small residence and the Walkups lived there until the Clark Homes dwelling was repaired.

In 1960, Lawrence and Lucy Walkup moved to the new home for college presidents. The new President's House had a mixed design, incorporating elements of the Bungalow and Ranch architectural styles. When the Walkups moved to a new home in University Heights in 1975, the President's House became the Hospitality House, which served a variety of university functions, including as the faculty club, which moved from the second floor of the Gammage Building.

In 1988, a nineteen-room wing was added to the structure. Three rooms became VIP mini-suites, often used for visiting ABOR members. The entire structure became The Inn at NAU and opened on June 10, 1989. The inn served as the campus restaurant and hotel until 2008. The lodging wing is in a modern International style with a Colonial Revival entrance. The restaurant opened for breakfast, lunch, and, for some periods, weekday dinners. It had a small bar, full kitchen, and conference room. An outdoor patio and the Golden Eagle Lounge opened in 1989. Students from the Eugene M. Hughes School of Hotel and Restaurant Management augmented a professional staff, gaining firsthand experience in all facets of the hospitality business.

In late 2008, the inn closed. The new High Country Conference Center and Drury Inn & Suites provide the training and internship functions previously provided on campus. Renovations, costing about $3 million, modified the structure to become offices, classrooms, and laboratory space for the Hughes School of Hotel and Restaurant Management.

Left: View of the President's House in the early 1960s.

Below: The Inn at NAU (2008), shortly before conversion to classrooms, offices, and laboratory space for the School of Hotel and Restaurant Management.

Home Management House/ Arizona Hospitality Research and Resource Center

Home management, domestic science, domestic arts, and home economics were names for part of the curriculum for nearly seven decades. The discipline involved training women in the skills needed to be homemakers and to enable them to instruct high school students. The curriculum included cooking, sewing, child care, and other subjects. Originally, classes met in Old Main and remained there as late as 1953. When the new Technology and Applied Arts Building (the Communications Building) opened in 1961, the instructional component moved there and gradually merged into other subject areas, coinciding with societal changes and the decline in the need for high school teachers of home economics.

In addition to classroom instruction, home economics required a location for practicing the various skills. It is unclear where the original Home Management House was located. By 1920, a planned renovation of Herrington House, moved from the hill where the Blome Building stands to a place near the Riles Building, would make this the Home Management House. President McMullen chose to save costs and used the funds to renovate the structure as a home for the school's presidents. The practical aspects of home economics took place in a small cottage located between the infirmary and a greenhouse building, behind Taylor Hall.

In 1958, the state legislature approved $35,000 to construct a new Home Management House. Designed in the modern International tradition, accented by Chicago-style windows and a Craftsman-style entryway, the brick structure opened in 1961. The Home Management House retained its original purpose until 1973–1974, when home economics faded from the curriculum. For several years in the mid-1980s, the new Student Center and Alumni Relations occupied the building. In 1989, a $200,000 renovation added a laboratory wing and reconfigured the interior into offices and classrooms.

Later, this structure became the Arizona Hospitality Research and Resource Center (AHRRC). The AHRRC, operated in conjunction with the Hughes School of Hotel and Restaurant Management, provides information and advice for the tourism industry in Arizona, with particular emphasis on northern Arizona. A resource library serves students, faculty, and professionals, and AHRRC stages workshops for interested groups in subjects pertaining to the tourism industry. As the Hotel and Restaurant Management facilities undergo significant remodeling and expansion, this structure is scheduled for demolition.

Left: Home Management House (1961).

Below: Home Management House as the Arizona Hospitality Research and Resource Center (2008).

Eugene M. Hughes School of Hotel and Restaurant Management

The program in hotel and restaurant management began in 1986, growing from a need for training in various aspects of the travel and tourism industry. The Eugene M. Hughes School of Hotel and Restaurant Management (HRM) bears the name of the twelfth president of NAU, who played a critical role in establishing the unit. The main building opened in 1988, with the dedication on June 10, 1989. The School of HRM is part of a three-building complex that includes the Inn at NAU and the Arizona Hospitality Research and Resource Center. The highly ranked program has strong international enrollment, with students from more than twenty-five countries.

The structure is an example of postmodern architecture, including elements that echo the past without replicating history, as in some earlier Revival styles. The neoclassical elements in the entryway are one such feature. The HRM Building contains offices, classrooms, computer laboratories, a seminar area, and a lecture room.

The new High Country Conference Center and associated Drury Inn & Suites provide excellent opportunities for student training and internships. The former Inn at NAU, along with the current HRM Building, will become offices and state-of-the-art classrooms, including new laboratory spaces with special facilities for a culinary laboratory.

Biography

Eugene Morgan Hughes was born on April 3, 1934, in Scottsbluff, Nebraska. He began life during the Great Depression, an only child, with memories of a small apartment as home. Hughes worked summers on the farm owned by his maternal grandparents. He graduated from high school in 1952, attended Scottsbluff Junior College, and then obtained his bachelor of science in mathematics from Chadron State Teachers College (Chadron State University), located in northwest Nebraska. During high school and college, Hughes was an accomplished athlete and part of teams in football, basketball, baseball, and track. In 1958, he completed his master of science in the College of Agriculture and Applied Science at Kansas State University in Manhattan.

His first job was as a mathematics instructor at Chadron State. He became the department head and then assistant to the college president. From 1962 to 1968, Hughes studied at George Peabody College for Teachers in Nashville, Tennessee, completing his doctorate in 1968. He returned to Nebraska, rejoined the faculty at Chadron State, and served on the board of trustees for Nebraska State Colleges.

Eugene M. Hughes, twelfth president of NAU.

At the request of President Walkup, Hughes came to Flagstaff in 1970 to fill the position of dean of arts and sciences. He moved upward in administration, to academic vice president in 1977 and president of Northern Arizona University in 1979. Perhaps his most significant contribution was the expansion of the "hidden" infrastructure for the campus. The major expansions of the previous two decades burdened the aging, inadequate heating, water, and other service systems of the campus. Hughes secured funding to update and expand these systems and to bury power lines, providing the open views the campus enjoys today. He presided over the Cline Library addition, the birth of the School of HRM, and the beginning of the NAU campus

at Yuma. He was a central figure in improving relations between the university and the local community and was Flagstaff Citizen of the Year in 1988.

Hughes was president of NAU for fourteen years; he accepted the presidency at Wichita State University in Kansas in 1993. When he retired from Wichita State in 1998, he and his wife returned to Flagstaff, where they reside today. In addition to the academic school named in his honor at NAU, the Eugene M. Hughes Metropolitan Complex, a conference and meeting center in Wichita, bears his name. Hughes was a member of the Arizona State Board of Education and served as its president; he was also chair of the American Association of State Colleges and Universities.

Eugene M. Hughes School of Hotel and Restaurant Management (2008).

Science Building/ Physical Sciences Building

The Science and Mathematics Departments moved from Old Main to Hanley Hall in 1935–1936. From there they moved to Frier Hall, designed to house the Science Department, in 1948. By the late 1950s, they had outgrown that space. A new structure arose on the site of the former Skidmore Field. This building, which still has the word "Science" inscribed in the stone above the west-side main entrance, opened in spring 1962 as home for the Science Division. The division eventually split into the Departments of Biology, Geology, Chemistry, Physics, and Mathematics. The Science Building was the first of four interconnected structures completed during the next decade, including additional science facilities and the Liberal Arts Building.

The 1959 state legislature provided funding for the building, which is textbook International style in design with ribbon windows and flat, gray spandrel panels. The interiors of this and the other buildings in this complex are purely functional and very similar—what one might call 1960s academic interior design with long corridors lacking exterior lighting and office and classroom doors arrayed along the length of each corridor. In 1961, the state provided an additional $100,000 to equip the new building.

Today, the Physical Sciences Building houses the Department of Physics and Astronomy and the Center for Environmental Sciences and Education. Within the Department of Physics and Astronomy are the National Undergraduate Research Observatory Program, shared with Lowell Observatory, and the National Aeronautics and Space Administration (NASA) undergraduate research program. The enduring relationship with Lowell Observatory has proved beneficial for both parties. Percival Lowell founded the observatory in 1894, a few years before the opening of Northern Arizona Normal School. Both research scientists and students share the resources at Lowell Observatory and on the NAU campus, resulting in research collaborations and shared external support for scholarly and training activities.

In the late 1960s, location changes by science departments began. The Departments of Biology and Chemistry moved to their own buildings in 1967 and 1968, respectively. Geology moved to Frier Hall and then to the U.S. Forest Service Building (now the Geology Annex) in 1992, when the Southwest Forest Science Complex opened. The Department of Geography moved to the Chemistry Building by 1970, and later to South Campus. Also housed in the Science Building for a time was the Department of Philosophy. Additional occupants included faculty and programs from Sociology, Nursing, and Anthropology.

Science Building (1960), which housed all the science departments, soon after completion.

Physical Sciences Building (2008).

Communications Building

The Communications Building was dedicated on April 1, 1961, as the School of Technology and Applied Arts. The structure faced north and was in the modern International style. At the time, academic units in the building included home economics on the second floor and industrial education on the first floor, with fine arts located on the third floor. Home economics included fashion, merchandising, foods and nutrition, and interior design. By 1967, art, speech, and drama were all located in the Applied Arts Building, along with the early engineering curriculum, which grew, in part, from the industrial education program. Portions of the Music Department resided in this building as well as in Old Main and the Liberal Arts Building. By 1970, the designation became the School of Applied Science and Technology and some years later the Art and Design Building, with home economics, industrial arts, and engineering and technology. The Department of Police Science and Administration joined this school in 1971, though it was physically located in the Liberal Arts Building.

Several special features characterized the building. A bay with associated door was located on the first floor in the industrial education space. A house, built by the students in this curriculum, was moved to a location on Kingman Street in Flagstaff in 1983. A carillon installed in Old Main was turned off when the building became a men's residence hall; the students complained about the noise. On December 6, 1973, the refurbished carillon was heard from a new location atop the Applied Arts Building. The carillon later moved to the top of the Activity Center, and more recently it was relocated to the North Union.

In the 1990s, a modest series of renovations, costing about $1.2 million, provided Interactive Instructional Television (IITV) classrooms and studios. In 2001, a major renovation altered the building dramatically. The Communications Building today faces south with a sweeping glass entrance, balcony, and a wall with the First Amendment Plaza. The remodeled structure is in postmodern architecture style, but without much stylistic structure. It has an environmental design with passive solar heating, and many curves and angles.

The building has been home to the School of Technology and Applied Arts, School of Journalism, College of Design and Technology, School of Applied Sciences, portions of the College of Creative and Communication Arts, and School of Communications. Formed in fall 1984, the School of Communications became part of the College of Social and Behavioral Sciences in 2004. The Communications Building houses NAU's Television Services operations, classrooms, studios for art and photography, and offices, along with the *Lumberjack* student campus newspaper and KJACK, the on-campus student radio station. In late summer 2008, construction commenced on a sizable addition to the Communications Building to provide new, expanded space for the NAU Distance Learning operations, currently housed in the Blome Building.

Main entrance to the School of Technology and Applied Arts (ca. 1970),
with Lumberjack Gym and Liberal Arts visible to the left.

Opposite: South-facing view of the Communications Building
(1970s), showing the balcony over the classroom wing.

122

Newly renovated south-facing entrance to the Communications Building (2008), showing the First Amendment Plaza.

North side of the Communications Building (2008).

Lumberjack Stadium/ Spilsbury Field

The first athletic field for organized sports activity at Northern Arizona Normal School was McMullen Field (ca. 1923). Skidmore Field, located in the area where the science buildings are today, replaced McMullen Field in 1933. In 1937, W. H. Waggoner, president of the Arizona Livestock Company, gave the college twenty-eight acres east of the campus; these became Waggoner Fields, where sports were played until the 1970s.

Arizona State College experienced rapid growth during the 1940s and 1950s. As plans unfolded for construction of the Science and Liberal Arts Buildings, a new athletic facility was needed. In 1956, the state legislature provided funding for a remodel and relocation of the existing stadium structure and field lighting at Skidmore Field. The cost was $276,000; Weeks Construction Company handled the operations and Arizona House Moving Company handled the actual move. The stadium made its journey in January 1957, with twenty-two sets of dollies and four hundred tons of steel and concrete transferred from Skidmore Field to the area designated for Lumberjack Stadium. After completing the track and field facilities, and allowing two years for the turf to mature, the first football game at Lumberjack Stadium occurred in 1960. The ASC squad defeated the Fort Huachuca Army Base team, 47–0. The stands, open

to the elements at Skidmore Field, were given a roof and three side walls in 1961. In fall 2008, the field at Lumberjack Stadium was renamed Max Spilsbury Field to honor the longtime head football coach.

Lumberjack Stadium opened with a seating capacity of approximately 4,300, which in fall 1965 increased to 8,500. Natural grass was later replaced with an artificial surface made of all-weather, high-quality polyurethane. The stadium is used primarily for soccer and track and field.

Space beneath the stadium on the west side houses the NAU Police Department and the Center for High Altitude Training. The NAUPD is a fully accredited police operation today. The earliest campus security consisted of a night watchman, with local police handling campus crime. By the 1960s, the campus had a Security Division, housed within the physical plant facilities in the Plateau Center. The Security Division relocated briefly to the former President's House (Herrington House), and then in 1977 to a structure on the knoll by the Atmospheric Research Observatory. The NAU Police Department has been in its current location beneath Lumberjack Stadium since 1984.

The Center for High Altitude Training was an outgrowth of interest in the benefits of training at higher elevations. This type of training began to be seen before

Bleachers for Lumberjack Stadium were moved from Skidmore Field on rollers during the winter of 1956–1957.

the 1968 Mexico City Olympics and became popular in the ensuing decades. In 1994, the idea of a high-altitude training center was formalized. Facilities were initially located in the Recreation Center but were moved to a remodeled location at Lumberjack Stadium in 1997. In 2006, the center was designated as an Official Olympic Training Site. The center sponsored a number of programs including the Native American Running Program, Flagstaff Running Project, and the Team Altius Youth Scholarships. It closed in early 2009 because of budget issues.

Biography

Max Spilsbury was born on June 16, 1924. He boxed and played football for the University of Arizona Wildcats in the late 1940s, and served in the U.S. Marines, where he received combat wounds, including a serious injury to one knee. He was head football coach at NAU (then called Arizona State College) from 1956 to 1962. He left NAU to become a school superintendent and coach in Bisbee. An inspirational coach, he was inducted into the Arizona Football Hall of Fame in 1971. He died on November 21, 2001, in El Paso, Texas. Sam Borozan, an administrator and booster of the NAU Athletics Hall of Fame, established the Max Spilsbury Scholarship in 1986.

Max Spilsbury, former NAU head football coach. In 2008, the field at Lumberjack Stadium was named in his honor.

Opposite: Lumberjack Stadium (1958), prior to the addition of the roof and walls for the bleachers.

Under the west side of Lumberjack Stadium are facilities for the NAU Police Department and the former Center for High Altitude Training.

Lumberjack Stadium (2007) with the San Francisco Peaks in the background.

Business Administration Building/ Adel Mathematics Building

Authorization for, and construction of, a new business building occurred in 1961, using an appropriation of $800,000. It is in the same style as the Eastburn Education Building and is a good example of postwar modern or International architecture. With only minor changes, including the addition of an elevator, the building remains much the same today as when it opened. The exception is renovated space that is used as an Interactive Instructional Television (IITV) classroom and studio. In 1984 the Business Administration Building was renamed the Adel Mathematics Building, in honor of Arthur Adel.

The building opened in 1962 as the first independent home for the business administration curriculum. Previously, commercial and business classes were taught in other campus buildings, most notably in Old Main and Gammage. The Department of Psychology resided in the Adel Building from the late 1970s through the early 1980s. This move occurred after Business Administration moved to new quarters on South Campus, but before the Psychology Department moved to the College of Social and Behavioral Sciences in 1982. In 1981, the Department of Psychology was divided between two schools: Educational Psychology remained with Education, and Clinical Psychology became a separate department, housed in what is now Adel. For a time in the early 1980s, this building was referred to as Education East.

The introduction of the first computer on campus, in 1964, occurred in this building.

Unknown by many, there is a small apartment located at the south end of the Adel Building. Several NAU presidents and other administration officials used the apartment as a temporary residence and it served as lodging for guests on the campus.

Demonstrating the power of a business degree from an earlier era, a 1974 alumnus, Ron Heil, set a world record by typing for 162 hours and 1 minute. An NAU College of Business Administration graduate and typing teacher at Burroughs High School in California, Heil typed 343,980 words on 910 pages for the record.

Opposite: Front entrance of the Business Administration Building (late 1960s).

Biography

Arthur Adel was born on November 22, 1908, in Brooklyn, New York. Raised in Brooklyn and Detroit, Michigan, he did undergraduate and graduate studies at the University of Michigan. His bachelor's degree involved a double major in physics and mathematics. His early work and doctoral thesis were at the crossroads between the two disciplines. His major emphasis was application of physics and mathematics to astronomy. While completing his graduate study, he worked from 1933 to 1935 at Lowell Observatory in Flagstaff. He spent 1935–1936 as a postdoctoral fellow at Johns Hopkins University in Baltimore.

Adel returned to Lowell Observatory in 1936 and remained until 1942. During World War II, he taught at the University of Michigan and conducted research for the U.S. Navy and Office of Scientific Research and Development. From 1946 to 1948, Adel was an assistant professor at the McMath-Hulbert Solar Observatory near Lake Angelus, Michigan. In 1948, he and his wife, Catherine, returned to Flagstaff, where he joined the NAU faculty in astronomy. He served until 1976, when he retired. Adel was the first NAU faculty member to attain international stature through important research contributions. He played a significant role in the development of planetary astronomy—his work in astrophysics encompassed studies of the chemical composition of planets' atmospheres, and he pioneered the use of infrared spectroscopy for planetary

investigations. Adel was one of only sixteen speakers chosen for the centennial meetings of the Royal Meteorological Society in the United Kingdom in 1950.

At NAU, Adel was the lead person in obtaining the Atmospheric Research Observatory, which became operational in 1952; supported by the U.S. Air Force, it was originally the Air Force Atmospheric Observatory. During the 1960s, Adel was a host for the NASA astronauts when they visited northern Arizona to use the lava fields and Meteor Crater for training exercises in preparation for lunar exploration. In 1982, he was influential in the establishment of the NAU chapter (then a club) of Sigma Xi, the national science honor society. Adel was a Fellow of the American Physical Society and a member of the Explorers Club and the Arizona Academy of Science. After his retirement in 1976, Adel remained in Flagstaff, where he died on September 13, 1994.

Arthur Adel.

Front entrance of the Adel Mathematics Building (2008).

McDonald Hall

The North Apartments (Apartment Units North) opened in 1962, housing 110 students. In 1989, President Hughes renamed the building in honor of Lewis J. McDonald, a longtime member of the university community, known as Mr. Lumberjack for his ardent support of the school and its athletic teams. McDonald Hall is located between the University Union and the NAU Bookstore and exhibits modern International architecture. Today, it is a coeducational dormitory. In the middle to late 1960s, McDonald Hall was, for a time, home to several sororities (Old Sorority Dorm); these moved to Raymond Hall in fall 1967. In the late 1960s, McDonald Hall was home to at least one fraternity.

There is a central courtyard, adding to the sense of community for this relatively small housing unit. The Campus Escort Service, which operates in cooperation with the NAU Police Department in assisting students and faculty who are walking between campus locations in the evening, has its home in McDonald Hall.

Biography

Lewis J. (Lewie) McDonald was born on October 29, 1906, in Butte, Montana. The McDonalds were miners and moved to Jerome, Arizona, in 1917. Lewis graduated from Jerome High School in 1926 and enrolled at NASTC in fall 1927. He was twice elected student body president during his undergraduate years. In March 1930, he had the honor of introducing the director of Lowell Observatory, Dr. C. O. Lampland, to a student assembly; Lampland announced the recent discovery of Pluto.

After receiving his bachelor of arts in education (1931), McDonald was a teacher, school principal, and superintendent of schools for twenty years in Jerome. He served as the elected mayor of Jerome during 1950–1951. He earned his master's degree at ASC and moved to Flagstaff in 1952, to work at his alma mater. He took a leave of absence in 1957 to organize and serve as the first principal and superintendent of a new school system in Page, stimulated by a growing population associated with construction of the Glen Canyon Dam.

Returning from Page, McDonald continued a long and productive association with NAU. He taught in the education program, eventually becoming director of Student Placement, assisting students seeking employment and conducting outreach to public schools in Arizona. He was on the first board of directors for the NAU Foundation and chaired the committee that arranged President Lawrence Walkup's inauguration. In 1956, he completed his doctoral degree at the University of Southern California. In 1969, NAU students conferred upon Lewis the honorary title "Mr. Lumberjack."

From 1958 until the early 1970s, McDonald was the director of University Relations. He served as mentor to a number of younger NAU colleagues, most notably Robert Crozier, who aided the university over five decades in capacities related to development and public outreach. McDonald, elected president of the Alumni Association in 1938, was given an honorary degree from his alma mater forty years later (1979).

Lewis McDonald retired from NAU in 1976. He entered politics, winning election as state senator. In 1989, the North Apartments became McDonald Hall. He retired to Gallup, New Mexico, in 1990, where he died on April 29, 1995.

Lewis J. McDonald.

McDonald Hall (2008).

136

Raymond Hall

The residence hall named for Dr. R. O. Raymond opened in 1962 to accommodate an increase in enrollment. It has a modern International style, similar to Tinsley, Cowden, and McDonald Halls. Raymond Hall has apartment-style living quarters and, reminiscent of Gillenwater Hall, there is a balustrade on the second story, characteristic of motel-style architecture of the period.

Raymond served as a home for the sororities at NAU from the late 1960s until Mountain View Hall opened in 1990. Today, Raymond Hall is coeducational and accommodates 270 students. Its residents are both undergraduates and graduate students. Raymond's central location, with close proximity to the University Union, bookstore, and North Campus, is favored by many students. Like other dormitories in the Central Campus area, it has an interior courtyard for social and recreational activities.

Biography

Ralph Oliver Raymond was born on September 5, 1876, in rural Clinton County, Illinois, and died on July 6, 1959, in Flagstaff. His early education was in Illinois, where he obtained his medical degree at Washington University in St. Louis in 1899. He practiced medicine in St. Louis for several years, moved to Williams, Arizona, in 1904 for health reasons, and then moved to Flagstaff in 1908 to establish a medical practice. He opened a clinic and hospital in a large house located near the Arizona Lumber and Timber Company at the south end of town and chose 9 Leroux Street as the site for a building that served as both office and home.

Raymond was a humanitarian and philanthropist. It was common for him to treat patients free of charge, or teach them the health benefits of good nutrition and a balanced diet. Drs. Raymond and Martin Fronske, another prominent Flagstaff-area physician whose name also graces an NAU building (see Fronske Student Health Center), spent many days and nights providing medical care during the flu epidemic of 1918; neither of them contracted the disease. He was a judicious and prescient investor, purchasing large parcels of land around Flagstaff that became quite valuable. He traded land with the Forest Service for space for the Flagstaff Community Hospital. He donated large tracts of land for the good of the community, including Lindberg Springs south of Flagstaff and the land for the old Flagstaff Armory.

In 1951, Raymond established the Flagstaff Education Foundation. At his death in 1959, the foundation received his bequest of a substantial amount of land (worth an estimated $300,000), stocks, and cash. The organization was renamed the Raymond Foundation and continues to award scholarships to qualified Coconino County high school students who attend NAU.

Dr. R. O. Raymond and his corgis.

Opposite: Raymond Hall as a student dormitory. Though similar, north and south ends of McDonald and Raymond Halls are not true mirror images.

Raymond Hall (2008).

Campus Heights Apartments

(One Part No Longer Standing)

The Campus Heights Apartments are at the southeast corner of the intersection of Knoles and University Drives. They developed in two stages: The first phase of single-story apartments opened in 1963; the second phase of two-story, two-bedroom apartments concluded the project in 1965. The complex replaced outdated temporary housing units (Splinter City).

Demolition of the single-story units in 2004 made room for McKay Village. The remaining section of Campus Heights, initially called Dorm J, consists of eight two-story buildings containing twenty-eight one-bedroom and fifty-four two-bedroom apartments. The buildings are in the modern International style, with nothing really of note to distinguish them—a trademark of the style being its actual lack of stylistic ornamentation. Today, the structures house married couples with children and single parents.

Early photograph of Campus Heights, as single-story apartments.

Oblique aerial view of Campus Heights showing single-story apartments (removed in 2004) and two-story apartments, with Mount Williams in the far distance to the west.

Interior courtyard and play area of Campus Heights Apartments (2008).

Liberal Arts Building

The Liberal Arts Building opened in 1964. Like other buildings completed on North Campus during the 1960s, it is textbook International style with ribbon windows and gray spandrel panels. Significant renovations, costing $800,000, occurred during the past twenty-five years, resulting in upgrades and refurbishment as well as the accommodation of Interactive Instructional Television (IITV).

Numerous academic units occupied this structure, including the three current residents—the Departments of English and History and the Martin-Springer Institute. Social science, which consisted of both history and political science, was in the Liberal Arts Building until the Social and Behavioral Sciences Building opened on South Campus. Other tenants were the Departments of Philosophy, Modern Languages, and Police Science (Criminal Justice); Latin American Civilizations; and the Army ROTC program. At the time the building opened it housed the largest lecture hall on campus. This room, referred to as LA 135, seats about one hundred people. It accommodates classes, guest lectures, faculty meetings, and student organizations. Renovations to offices and classrooms in portions of this building began in summer 2007, starting with the fourth floor.

The Liberal Arts Building (1960s), with Powers Drive in the foreground and the Science Building in the background.

Liberal Arts Building (2008).

Cowden Learning Community

In January 1964, Cowden Hall opened with space for more than four hundred women. Originally Dorm F, it is designed in the modern International style. When campus expansion shifted southward in the decades following its construction, Cowden Hall ended up near the center of campus.

Today, Cowden Learning Community is coed with 416 students. It is home for the NAU Honors and Three Year Degree Programs. Established in 1958, the Honors Program has had many homes in its half century of existence, including Cline Library, the Biology Building, the current Employee Assistance and Wellness House on South Beaver Street, the Public and Environmental Service Building on South Campus, and Old Main.

In an unprecedented expansion for the campus, this structure was one of six dedicated in 1964: Cowden and Tinsley Halls, the Liberal Arts Building, the Business Administration Building (Adel), Campus Heights Apartments, and a new South Dining Hall (Gateway Center). The Cowden Leaning Community has a classroom facility and a computer laboratory, and its residents excel in their involvement on campus and in the larger Flagstaff community.

Biography

James Steele Cowden was born on September 11, 1851, in a log cabin in rural Greene County, Missouri. His parents were natives of Tennessee and immigrated to Missouri in 1842. His father died soon after his son's birth, leaving a widow and three children. Cowden grew up on the family homestead, which his mother maintained for some years. At age eighteen, he began buying out family heirs and remained owner of the homestead until 1893, raising livestock and operating a sawmill.

After living briefly in Springfield, Missouri, he inhabited several farms in southwest Missouri. During this period, James Cowden purchased a sizable tract of land in northern Arizona. He exchanged 320 acres of this land with ASC for a parcel of forested land located near campus. He spent parts of each year in Arizona, raising alfalfa and cattle. He died at his home in Missouri.

James S. Cowden (left), shown here with his wife and John G. Babbitt at the dedication of the building.

Cowden Hall (late 1960s).

Cowden Learning Community (2008).

Tinsley Hall

Tinsley and Cowden Halls were built in 1964. Not surprisingly, both buildings share similar architecture and are in the modern International style. Tinsley Hall houses 410 students. In the past, it served as single-sex housing for females or males. During the years 1995–1997, expenditures of approximately $750,000 resulted in renovations to public spaces and modifications to accommodate the Office of International Programs.

Two special programs call Tinsley Hall home. The Modern Language House was created for students wishing to converse in a language other than English, most notably French, German, and Spanish. The Office of International Programs, at the north end of the building, manages processes for NAU students who study abroad and is responsible for assisting foreign students who come to NAU.

Biography

William Tinsley was born on December 26, 1891, in White Stone, South Carolina. He received his early education at local schools in South Carolina and earned bachelor of arts degrees in English and history from Columbia Union College in Takoma Park, Maryland, in 1920. He attended George Washington University in Washington, D.C., for graduate studies and received his master's degree in history and international relations in 1925 from Clark University in Worcester, Massachusetts.

Tinsley moved to Crested Butte, Colorado, where he was school superintendent for two years. He came to NASTC in 1927 and remained on the faculty and in various administrative capacities for thirty-five years. He was a teacher of social studies, history, and English. He headed the social studies unit—later the Department of History. While on the faculty, he received his doctorate from Stanford University. From 1928 to 1947, he was variously dean of men and head resident in Taylor and Bury Halls, served as campus coordinator with the U.S. Navy for the V-12 cadets, and was director of instruction and then dean of the college from 1944 to 1947. He assumed the role of dean of the graduate council starting in 1947.

William Tinsley was the 1947 homecoming dedicatee. He was faculty adviser or sponsor for numerous campus organizations. Tinsley was active in local affairs, including terms as president of the Flagstaff Rotary Club and Community Concert Association. He died at home in Flagstaff on April 6, 1962.

William Tinsley, who held many faculty and administrative positions at NAU, including dean of men and, later, dean of the college.

Tinsley Hall (1964), near completion, with the San Francisco Peaks visible to the right.

Tinsley Hall (2008).

University Union Field House

The University Union Field House comprises four structures built over several decades and melded into a single structure serving multiple purposes related to student activities and organizations.

North Activity Center/Field House

The North Activity Center opened in 1965 with a modern International-style design. It has a Quonset hut appearance, with metal mullions, and International-style, plate-glass windows. Initially, it contained offices for coaches and staff, locker rooms, and a large indoor arena for track and field, volleyball, tennis, and baseball practice. The Department of Physical Education and Recreation called the North Activity Center (University Center) home. Land on which the

adjoining University Union sits had tennis courts accessible from the south side of the Activity Center. The building served as the venue for registration each semester, outfitted with tables and faculty advisers from each department. By the 1980s, computerized registration replaced this system, combined with individualized attention for students in their majors.

With the advent of other venues for athletics, including Walkup Skydome, Wall Aquatic Center, Rolle Activity Center, and the Recreation Center, functions of the renamed University Union Field House changed. The Kaibab Room on the lower level was a dining area, then a bowling alley, and now serves as a meeting room for university functions and outside groups. The upper level,

View of the North Activity Center (1965), later renamed University Union Field House.

much of which was a ballroom, became "Cowboy Town" in the late 1980s, with rustic touches and offices for student organizations and advisement. These included Native American Student Services, Upward Bound, Nizhoni Academy, and Student Support Services. In 2008, Native American Student Services, the Multicultural Student Center, and Educational Support Programs combined as Educational Support Services, still housed on the upper level of Field House.

Currently, campus food services operations have their headquarters on the first floor of Field House. The large indoor arena serves for recreation, intramural sports, occasional team practices, and functions such as Career Day, science fairs, and expositions. Significant Field House renovations include $4 million in 1994–1996 for the second-floor changes. The appearance of Field House changed dramatically with the addition to the food services portion of the University Union, completed in summer 2008. Field House and the Kaibab Room house portions of recreation and associated programs owing to renovations and expansion of the Recreation Center that began in summer 2009.

Student Services

Student Services, the second phase of the University Union Field House combination, opened in 1987. The west portion of the combined structure, with space for student organizations, was constructed in an early postmodern style mixed with International-style elements. Aspects of the architectural styles include irregular rooflines, somewhat reminiscent of the earlier Craftsman style, and the use of cut brick. Much of this structure sits on land previously occupied by the Stone Cottages. Numerous student service functions were consolidated in this structure (which also houses the dean of students): the Office of Student Life, and Student Affairs with related offices including the Association of

University Residence Halls (AURH), Associated Students for Women's Issues (ASWI), and the Associated Students of Northern Arizona University (ASNAU).

The second floor has conference rooms of varying sizes to accommodate university activities and functions and to provide space for community groups. ABOR met in these rooms for many years, ending with the opening of the High Country Conference Center in 2008.

Food Services

Near the southern end of the 1961 campus, a new eating facility, Central Dining, opened. The facility served students residing in Gillenwater, Raymond, and McDonald Halls as well as those in Cottage City and Peterson and Babbitt Halls. The University Union was large enough to accommodate commuter and off-campus residents. A variety of eating establishments in this facility came and went over several decades, some of the waited-service variety and others in the buffet style that became a staple of dining services at many universities in the 1970s.

In 1980, after extensive remodeling, a food services section was added east of and incorporating the original structure. Nearly $3 million in remodeling and renovations over the past two decades (1990–2010) upgraded infrastructure systems due to changing food services needs. Also housed in the University Union are the Central Ticket Office, Sun Entertainment, and Dining Card and ID Card Administration.

There were additional modifications in summer 2007, and a significant addition to the University Union's west side opened in fall 2008. The design, by O'Donnell, Wicklund, Pigozzi, and Peterson, was built by Kinney Construction at a cost of $9.5 million. This structure, with its sweeping style and glass facade, has new eateries, a second level with lounge areas, and two balconies. As NAU moves toward becoming a green campus, features of this

152

expansion project will include a location where students can fill up water bottles with filtered water and the restrooms will feature recycled materials and water-saving devices.

Tennis Courts

The first tennis court was located at the foot of the front steps of Old Main. By 1930, this tennis court, with an asphalt surface, moved to the site now occupied by the North Union, where it remained until after World War II. An earlier sand tennis court occupied land north of Old Main beginning about 1915.

After World War II, tennis courts were found at a number of other locations. In the 1960s, and prior to the construction of the annex to the Biological Sciences Building, there were three courts just north of Babbitt and

Peterson Halls. At about the same time, there were three courts just east of Cowden and Tinsley Halls, approximately where Aspen Crossing dormitory opened in fall 2008; volleyball courts occupied this area for some years prior to the new dormitory. In the late 1960s, four courts were constructed south of the University Union Field House. Another set of tennis courts occupied land near McConnell Hall on South Campus. Enterprising students collected large pieces of cardboard and attached them to the fence surrounding these courts to block the wind that arose in late February and early March. On sunny days, they used this enclosed area for sunbathing. A set of tennis courts constructed northwest of Lumberjack Stadium in 1985 became a parking lot in 2006. The Field House has several indoor tennis courts.

Central Dining as it appeared in 1961, just before it opened for service.

University Union, view from the Central Dining side (2008), showing the original Central Dining structure as incorporated into the current structure.

New wing of the University Union, which opened in fall 2008. Note the portion of University Union Field House visible at the right side of the photograph.

Overflow Housing

Some years, more students enrolled at the college than could be housed in the existing dormitories. This resulted in a variety of creative measures to house the students. As noted elsewhere, buildings such as Herrington House and the Dairy Barn provided rooms for students. The Armory (now a furniture store) at the corner of Milton and Butler and a warehouse adjacent to the College Inn on Humphreys Street served as housing for men. All of these arrangements were temporary, generally lasting for anywhere from weeks to a full academic year.

There were fall semesters where double-occupancy rooms housed three students. The pressure for dormitory space lessened during the year as students either found other accommodations or left campus. Clark Homes, part of the historic area west of downtown Flagstaff, and nearby Barker Village sometimes served as student and faculty housing.

A common solution to the overcrowding problem was to use local motels. There were numerous motels in Flagstaff for summer tourist traffic. The college leased motels for the academic year or, in some instances, students rented directly from the proprietor. Among the many motels that housed students were the Arizona Motel, Auto Lodge, Flamingo Motel, Du Beau Motel, French Quarter, Imperial 400, Saga Motel, Rodeway Inn, Evergreen Motel, Hotel Monte Vista, and Time Motel. As recently as 1977, the Towne and Country Motel and Ramada Inn served for student housing. In fall 1980, rooms at the Evergreen Inn were leased; this ended in spring 1982.

Wilson Hall

Wilson Hall (Dorm H) opened in 1965. Today it is a coeducational residence for 430 students, with separate wings for men and women. Designed in a modern International style, the exposed pillars forming the front entrance are evidence of structural elements characteristic of this architecture style. One tradition at Wilson Hall has the name "Ugly Resident Assistant Contest." Students dress their resident assistants to make them supremely ugly, with a panel of residents judging the winner.

Biography

Charles B. Wilson Jr. was the son of a prominent Flagstaff attorney, Charles B. Wilson. Charles Jr.'s parents moved from Illinois in 1910 to the Glendale area, where they helped Mrs. Wilson's father farm for a year. Charles Sr. then moved his family north to Flagstaff to establish a law practice, which he continued for more than fifty years. Charles Jr. was born on September 14, 1913, in Flagstaff, attended Emerson School in town, then the Training School at Northern Arizona Normal School, and graduated from Flagstaff High School in 1930. As a side job, during his schooling, he assisted with setting up for various movies filmed in the area around Flagstaff during the late 1920s and well into the early 1930s. He attended Park College in Missouri for two years and obtained his law degree from the University of Arizona. Wilson began practicing law in Flagstaff in 1935, joining his father's firm. He served as a gunnery officer in the U.S. Navy on the USS *Essex* during World War II.

Wilson worked diligently during the 1940s to ensure survival of the college. Drastic enrollment declines during the war years were countered, in part, by the Navy V-12 unit on campus. He was instrumental in efforts to secure the right to grant liberal arts and science degrees. During the 1940s and 1950s, the institution transitioned from being a teacher preparatory school to one with a broader mission.

Professionally, Wilson was Coconino County attorney, superior court judge, attorney for the Santa Fe Railroad, and served a term as president of the Arizona State Bar Association in 1940. He was a charter member of the Rotary Club and a leading figure in Flagstaff. Wilson received an honorary degree from Arizona State College in 1960. Along with Lewis McDonald, Lawrence Walkup, and Martin Fronske, Wilson served on the first board of directors for the NAU Foundation. Charles B. Wilson Jr. died in 1990 in Flagstaff.

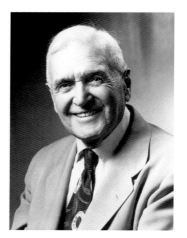

Charles B. Wilson Jr.

Opposite: Wilson Hall (late 1960s), shortly after opening.

Wilson Hall (2008).

Health Facilities and Fronske Student Health Center

Over the course of more than one hundred years, a variety of facilities served for managing students' health care. No evidence exists of an on-campus facility for student health in the earliest years. Those needing medical attention sought treatment in the Flagstaff community.

In 1926, an isolation hospital was constructed to keep contagious diseases from infecting the campus community. This cottage, referred to as the "Pest House," was located just south of the Power Plant Building and Taylor Hall. The cottage served originally as an overflow residence for students.

Renovations in 1932 extended the life of the facility for another five years. A new infirmary was built on the same site and is visible on maps and aerial photographs into the 1950s, north of Lumberjack Gym, but by 1959 it disappears from campus maps.

In 1960, an infirmary opened on the north side of Dupont Street, opposite North Hall, where the High Country Conference Center parking garage is today. Called Moeur Infirmary, it was named for Dr. B. B. Moeur, the Arizona governor. Fronske Student Health Center replaced Moeur Infirmary in 1965.

Plans for a University Health Center began in the early 1960s and it opened in 1965. Formal dedication occurred on May 1, 1966, the same day that Arizona State College became Northern Arizona University. This structure represents International-style architecture at the height of its national popularity. In 1979, the building's name changed to honor longtime Flagstaff physician Martin G. Fronske. The health center included twenty-six beds, clinical facilities, and a pharmacy. Today, there are several observation rooms with beds, but patients with ailments requiring hospitalization are sent to Flagstaff Medical Center.

Former patient rooms serve as offices for doctors, nurses, and nurse practitioners. For a time, two prefabricated units were located northeast of the health center; these contained the Counseling and Testing Center. Those units moved to the knoll by the Atmospheric Research Observatory, where they served as research space for the Anthropology Department.

Another pair of mobile units, added in 2007 northeast of the Fronske Center, house administrative offices, freeing space in the existing structure for patient care. In 2008, planning began for an expanded health center in conjunction with expansion of the Recreation Center and the Counseling and Testing Center.

Moeur Infirmary (1960), located across Dupont Street and North Hall.

View of Fronske Student Health Center (1965) just as it opened, with the San Francisco Peaks in the background.

Fronske Student Health Center sponsors outreach and educational programs for students, including health education, stress management, preventive medicine, and weight control. Staff members visit residence halls to discuss these issues and provide information on alcohol and drug abuse.

Biographies

Benjamin Baker Moeur was born on December 22, 1869, in Dechard, Tennessee, and died in Tempe, Arizona, on March 16, 1937, just months after completing his second term as governor. He was a Texas cowboy for a time and then completed a medical degree in 1896 in Little Rock, Arkansas. He moved to Tempe, where he served as a country doctor and began several business ventures, including co-ownership of a hardware store. Moeur became the school physician for Arizona State Teachers College at Tempe in 1925, a position he held for almost a decade. A politician at heart, he served on the Tempe school board, the Arizona Constitutional Convention (1910), and the Board of Education for the Normal School at Tempe. He served two two-year terms as governor of Arizona (1933–1937) during the Great Depression. In addition to the infirmary at Flagstaff, a building at Arizona State University bears the Moeur name.

Martin George Fronske was born on December 9, 1883, in St. Louis, Missouri, to German immigrant parents. He attended schools in St. Louis and received his medical degree from Washington University in 1907. After an internship, Fronske began practicing medicine in his hometown. For health reasons, he and his wife moved to Albuquerque in 1912, and then to Flagstaff in 1914, where

he remained for the rest of his life. His patients consisted primarily of those injured at sawmills or while cutting timber in local forests. He acquired the moniker "Baby Doctor" because, over several decades, he attended, by his own estimate, more than two thousand births.

Fronske and R. O. Raymond were key figures in caring for local citizens at the time of the 1918 influenza epidemic. Fronske was civic minded and became a member of the first board of directors of the Raymond Foundation as well as the NAU Foundation board. One of his sons, Robert Fronske, became a well-known Flagstaff photographer, and his large collection of photographs was donated to the Special Collections and Archives at NAU; several photographs from the Fronske Collection appear in this book.

Fronske received many accolades and awards during his life, including the Northern Arizona Distinguished Service Award (1972), a Special Recognition Award from the Arizona Sports Hall of Fame (1972), and the Robbins Award from the Arizona Medical Association (1967). He received the first honorary doctorate granted by Arizona State College in 1958. Fronske was an active member in the Flagstaff community and a charter member and trustee of the Federated Community Church.

He retired in 1949 but returned in 1951, served the college until 1962, and, even after a second retirement, did athletic physicals until 1970, when he was eighty-seven years of age. He served the university for more than fifty years and was a fixture in Flagstaff for nearly sixty years. Martin Fronske died in Tempe on April 2, 1984, at one hundred years of age.

B. B. Moeur, former governor of Arizona.

Martin G. Fronske.

Fronske Student Health Center (2008).

Cline Library

By 1902, the first school library opened in Old Main. The first librarian arrived in 1912. By 1918, the library consisted of about 3,000 volumes, enlarging to 7,000 by 1921, at which time there was a small branch library in the Training School. A new library building (Gammage) debuted in 1930 at a cost of $130,000. Library stacks in the new facility could hold up to 40,000 volumes, allowing for expansion from the 18,000 in the collection when the building opened. There were 320 seats for students and others to use the library materials or study. Special Collections and Archives began in 1932 with a collection donated by Harold Colton, founder and director of the Museum of Northern Arizona.

In the 1930s, fiction titles rented for 3 cents per day and the first student library fee ($1) began, but the Great Depression dampened library growth. From 1939 to 1970, Althea Ragsdale served as librarian. By the late 1940s, book acquisitions were again growing, with more than 1,000 titles added per year.

In 1966, as the school became Northern Arizona University, a new library opened. That structure, designed in the modern International style, is incorporated into the present Cline Library. The new library housed the existing collection of 100,000 volumes, with room for expansion, and had seating to accommodate 1,600 patrons. The collection moved from the old library in the Gammage Building during a single week in April 1966. In just over ten years, more room was needed to accommodate the rapidly growing collection; a major addition opened in 1980, adding 50 percent more space.

Between 1980 and 1986, the collection increased from 814,000 volumes to about 1.2 million. Planning by Jean Collins, university librarian, and strong support from President Eugene Hughes resulted in a substantial increase in library staff and approval of bonding for a major addition. In April 1988, the university named the building in honor of Platt and Barbara Cline, who provided many years of support for the university and education.

When a major addition opened in mid-1992, Special Collections and Archives moved to Central Campus from South Campus, where it was located from 1977 to 1992. Today, Cline Library has almost 1.5 million volumes, with capacity for an additional 500,000. Both the 1980 and 1992 structures embody the postmodern architecture style, with large, square columns, a neoclassical entrance, and combinations of various materials for facades.

The past several decades witnessed changes in technology involving online card catalogs and electronic journals, plus many related services. The current departments within Cline Library are Content, Access and Delivery Services, Administration, Academic Course Support, Library Technology Services, Media Services, and Special Collections

College Library (late 1960s), with a portion of the Stone Cottages on the right and both the Eastburn Education Center and San Francisco Peaks visible in the center background.

and Archives. For several years in the 1990s, the NAU Honors Program was housed in Cline Library.

Biography

Platt Herrick Cline was born on February 7, 1911, in Mancos, Colorado, where he attended local schools, graduating from high school in 1928. He studied at New Mexico Military Institute at Roswell and attended the University of Colorado (Boulder) for a year. He met his wife, Barbara Decker, as a reporter for the *Mancos Times-Tribune*; they were married in 1936 and moved to Flagstaff in 1938. Cline served as a reporter for the *Denver Post*, Associated Press, and *Norwood Post-Independent* in Colorado and the *Coconino Sun* (precursor of the *Arizona Daily Sun*), *Winslow Mail*, and *Holbrook Tribune-News* in Arizona before assuming the editorship of the newly minted *Arizona Daily Sun* in 1946, a position he held for thirty years.

Platt and Barbara Cline worked as a team, particularly on local projects and causes. They were instrumental in early racial integration of the schools in Flagstaff. Platt was a strong supporter of education, including many efforts on behalf of Northern Arizona University. His sequential and sometimes overlapping tenures as editor, publisher, and president of the *Arizona Daily Sun* encompassed a period of transition for the university. From the late 1950s until Cline stepped down from his newspaper position in 1976, much of Central Campus and South Campus developed.

The Clines were great supporters of and advocates for everything about northern Arizona—the people, the environment, and local educational and cultural institutions. An *Arizona Daily Sun* editorial at the time of Cline's death stated, "Platt Cline's vision was an inclusive one that honored diversity and tolerance for new ideas."

Cline authored several works of history devoted to Flagstaff and Northern Arizona University, including *They Came to the Mountain: The Story of Flagstaff's Beginnings*

(1976) and *Mountain Campus: The Story of Northern Arizona University* (1983). All of the books were written after Cline left the newspaper; he remained very active in retirement.

As a boy, he regularly entered the small local library when it was closed by climbing through a window, to borrow books—which he always returned. Cline helped to refurbish the former President's Office in Old Main, particularly through his efforts to find and retrieve the original desk used by leaders on campus. He championed the siting of Page on the Arizona side of what was to become Glen Canyon Dam and Lake Powell, ensuring a prominent role for Flagstaff in the development of Page.

He received numerous awards for his work, including the Master Editor-Publisher and Golden Service Awards from the Arizona Newspaper Association, Flagstaff Citizen of the Year in 1976, and an honorary degree from NAU in 1966. The library was named in honor of Platt and Barbara Cline in 1988. Barbara Cline, who was Flagstaff Citizen of the Year in 1996, died on June 15, 2001, in Flagstaff. Platt Cline died in Flagstaff on October 3, 2001.

Platt Cline, in his office at the **Arizona Daily Sun,** *surrounded by reference materials.*

Opposite: University Library (1970s).

Cline Library (2008) front entrance.

Sechrist Hall

At nine stories high, Sechrist Hall (Dorm K) opened for the 1966–1967 school year as the tallest building on campus, with housing for 608 male students. Its modern International style, with a stone facade, provides a commanding appearance. In fall 2000, Sechrist became a coeducational residence hall with men and women on alternate floors. It is home to a number of programs for freshmen and the transition to college life. Included in the facilities are a Resource Center; Office of Orientation, Transition, and Retention Services; several classrooms; separate study rooms; and a computer center, all remodeled in 2007.

Biography

Charles William Sechrist was born on February 2, 1896, in Meriden, Kansas, where he graduated from high school in 1914. He completed premedical studies at the University of Kansas and received his medical degree there in 1926. After a residency in St. Louis, Sechrist moved to Flagstaff. In 1935, he was a principal founder of the sixty-bed Flagstaff Hospital, which he gave to the city in 1955.

Sechrist worked closely with ASTCF in the late 1920s and early 1930s, and was the first president of the NAU Foundation, beginning in 1959. He was active in local affairs and served for eighteen years on the Flagstaff school board, fifteen of those years as president. For many years, he was the team physician for Flagstaff High School. Sechrist was a founding member of the Arizona School Boards Association. In 1940, he helped organize the Arizona Hospital Association. He served as a comissaryman in the U.S. Navy on the destroyer USS *Warrington* during World War II.

Sechrist Hall and three other locations in Flagstaff bear his name—a local public primary school, a wing of the Flagstaff Medical Center, and the Atrium of the Flagstaff Medical Center.

He received an honorary doctorate of education from Arizona State College in 1962. He died in Flagstaff on July 5, 1965. At the time of his death, he was speaker pro tem for the Arizona House of Representatives, serving his second term as representative from Coconino County.

Charles Sechrist, local physician and civic leader, with his wife at the dedication of Sechrist Hall.

West side of Sechrist Hall (2008) with the addition that is home for campus tours and a portion of Student Recruitment.

*Opposite: West side of Sechrist Hall (1970), with the
Gateway Center in the front left of the photograph.*

Biology Building

By the late 1950s, discussions had begun concerning a new structure for the Biology Department, but this effort stalled. With the granting of university status in 1966 and introduction of the doctoral program for biology, efforts were reignited and moved forward rapidly. The Biology Building opened in fall 1967, with formal dedication in November 1968 along with the new Chemistry Building. Speakers for the dedication ceremonies included William F. Libby, Harrison Schmitt, Lodewijk Dekker, and S. Charles Kendeigh, all world-renowned scientists. The architecture is textbook International style, with ribbon windows and gray spandrel panels. Initially, the Department of Mathematics occupied the first floor and the Department of Biology used the upper three floors of the building.

One story about the construction involves a phone call from Phoenix. James Wick, then chair of the department, was preparing the final design for the three-story structure when President Walkup phoned from the state legislature to inform him that he had secured funding for a fourth floor. What to do? After some quick justification for the funds, based on using the space for research that included undergraduates, the decision was to add the "new" floor between the second and third floors of the original plan. So, today's fourth floor of the Biology Building really was designed as the third floor.

Prior to 1968, the Biology Department occupied various campus locations. Originally, science classes were offered in Old Main; then sciences moved to quarters in Hanley Hall and later Frier Hall. The new building represented the Biology Department's first home designed with its needs in mind. Subsequently, portions of the Department of Biological Sciences moved to the Wettaw Biology and Biochemistry Building, the New Laboratory Facility, and the Applied Research and Development Building. Beginning in the early 1970s, when the South Academic Center was established, some biological scientists were located there as part of the health sciences curriculum, returning to North Campus in 1983.

In addition to the Department of Mathematics, other units housed in this structure include the Philosophy Department, the Center for Science Teaching and Learning (CSTL), and the Office of the Dean, first for the College of Arts and Sciences and, more recently, for the College of Engineering, Forestry, and Natural Sciences. Portions of Anthropology, Sociology, and Nursing, and all of Political Science, used the Biology Building at various times.

Biology Annex

Animal research on campus was first housed in the Psychology Laboratory, which is now the Counseling and Testing Center. In addition, a small facility for animal rearing was housed in the Liberal Arts Building. With the expansion of life sciences, it became evident that NAU needed a dedicated animal facility. Plans were made to construct what was called Bilby II, but gave way to the Biology Annex (also known as the Animal Quarters or Vivarium), which opened in 1989. This facility is equipped to house and care for a number of types of animals. Since the mid-1980s, all work with living animals adheres to very strict guidelines regulated by the federal government and enforced by a local committee of scientists and members of the Flagstaff community.

Biology Greenhouse

The Biology Greenhouse, accessed from the Liberal Arts Building, began service in 1971. The teaching greenhouse is separate from the South Campus Greenhouse Complex, which is used primarily for research. The teaching facility houses a variety of plants used in classes in introductory and plant biology classes.

Opposite: Biology Building courtyard (late 1960s).

West entrance of the Biological Sciences Building (2008).

Left: Biological Sciences Build-ing and Biology Annex (2008), with the San Francisco Peaks and top of the New Laboratory Facility in the background.

Below: Biology Greenhouse (2008), with the Liberal Arts Building in the background.

NAU Bookstore

The NAU Bookstore, built primarily in the International style and incorporating brick and cement, opened in 1967. Evidence suggests that, early on, students purchased books and class supplies at several locations, including Old Main, and from a private bookseller who maintained a shop just east of Campbell Hall for a time. Joe Rolle, returning to campus in 1947 from a position with the state government in Phoenix, managed the bookstore in the Gammage Building, where it was housed from the close of World War II until 1952, when the student union opened. The bookstore then moved there, where it remained for fifteen years.

In addition to the bookstore operations, a branch station of the U.S. Post Office is located in the basement of the building. Early postal services on campus involved visiting the Flagstaff post office to pick up mail for each building. Mail was placed on a table in the entryway of each building, where students claimed their letters and parcels from home. A small area with boxes for students was part of the new Union Building on North Campus; two students shared each box. The basement space in the new bookstore was designed specifically as a postal facility.

For some years, the school laundry and linen operations occupied portions of the basement of this building. Printing and Duplicating operations for the university shared space in the bookstore lower level with the post office, replacing the linen service in 1984.

A 1977 remodel doubled the available space, and a 1994 renovation provided for greater efficiency. Today, Follett Higher Education Group operates the bookstore; $1 million spent in summer 2007 provided major renovations.

The Lumberjack statue that stood at the west entrance of the NAU Bookstore is eight feet tall and depicts a handsome young man rather than the brawny, traditional view of a lumberjack. Cast in bronze by Charles Bonney, at the time an NAU student, the project involved many months of twenty-hour weeks, for which he was paid $1.70 an hour and, at the completion of the sculpture, an honorarium of $500. Bonney also produced the buffalo statue that adorns Buffalo Park in Flagstaff. A story, heard many times, holds that if a virgin female walks by the statue, the lumberjack will drop his axe. In 2008, the statue was moved to a location near the University Union Field House and dining facilities addition.

The west side of NAU Bookstore in 1967, before installation of the Lumberjack statue.

Right: East facade of NAU Bookstore (2008).

Below: The west entrance to NAU Bookstore in 2008, with the Lumberjack statue; the statue is now located between the Field House and the new wing of the University Union.

Gateway Student Success Center

Opened in 1967 as a much-needed additional dining facility, this structure has had several names, including South Dining Hall #2, University Avenue Dining, University Dining, and University Commons. The architecture is International, with an entryway added later, and a cupola and varied rooflines that provide an attractive appearance. In 2002–2003, a major renovation accompanied a change in function; the building became the Gateway Student Success Center. Remodeling resulted in offices, rooms for group meetings, a snack shop, and a resource library. Academic Advising, Premedical Professions, and Career Planning are housed here. The repurposing occurred after considerable study on the best way to assist students in obtaining information about classes and registration, seeking academic advice, and starting the processes involved in finding employment. Gateway Center is a success in terms of student recruitment and retention.

University Commons dining facility (1970s), with Sechrist Hall in the background.

Main entrance to Gateway Student Success Center (2008).

Allen Hall

Allen Hall (Dorm K) opened as the University Quadrangle, a residence for 460 women, in 1968. Designed in the modern International style, the name changed to Allen Hall in 1979 to honor longtime faculty member and university administrator Agnes Allen. Today, Allen Hall is a coeducational residence with men and women housed in different wings. Its location, not far from the center of campus, is advantageous in terms of access to classes, the library, and the University Union. Residents sponsor the annual campus-wide Woman of the Year recognition.

Biography

Agnes Allen was born in 1901 in Normal, Illinois, where her father was a high school biology teacher. When she was eight, the family moved to a farm in Missouri, where she grew up. They returned to Normal in 1918 when Agnes was a high school senior. She obtained a two-year teaching certificate from Illinois State Normal University (Illinois State University), with emphases in history and geography. Allen taught elementary school and then middle school. In 1924, she received her bachelor's degree in education and moved to Greeley, Colorado, completing a master of arts degree there in 1925. She found employment from 1925 to 1929 as a teacher at the Training School for Nebraska State College at Chadron. Allen then went to Hattiesburg, Mississippi, to teach geography at a small college. Owing to the Great Depression, out-of-state teachers at the school were released in 1932. She headed for Clark University in Worcester, Massachusetts, and obtained a second master's degree in 1934 and a doctoral degree in 1937, with fieldwork conducted in the Verde Valley in Arizona.

The college at Flagstaff needed someone to teach a five-week summer class in geography. Upon the recommendation of a friend of Allen's to President Tormey, Allen was offered the position. She came to Flagstaff in early summer 1934 and remained a part of the community for the rest of her life. Allen reached Flagstaff in 1934 by cross-country bus, traveling through Kansas in a horrendous dust bowl storm. During her exploration of the campus, she noted the small shacks located near the gymnasium (Riles)—the collapsible cabins purchased by President McMullen. On this first walk, she met Minnie Roseberry from the Training School; they became lifelong friends.

As a faculty member, Allen dedicated herself to training younger students to serve in elementary and secondary schools. Her specialties involved geography, geology, and science teaching methods. She soon joined the Science Department, located in Hanley Hall. She taught thirty-two different science courses over a career that spanned more than three decades.

Allen became the acting head of the sciences in 1943 and the position became permanent in 1946. During her long tenure with the sciences at the college, the size of the faculty in these disciplines increased from just three to fifty-three instructors. When the structure of the academic units changed, Allen became head of the Science Division.

She sometimes held other positions simultaneously, serving, for example, as director of Student Welfare in 1946 while leading the sciences. A pioneer as a female geographer, she was well known for the student field trips into the Grand Canyon every year, from 1936 until 1960.

Agnes Allen retired from Northern Arizona University in 1972, but remained in the Flagstaff area, where she died

Agnes Allen.

in 1995. Her honors include a Meritorious Service Recognition from the American Red Cross for volunteer efforts during World War II, election as a Fellow of the Arizona Academy of Science, recognition as an Outstanding Civic Leader in America, and election to Phi Kappa Phi. She was president of the Arizona Education Association in 1949, and president of the Arizona chapter of the American Association of University Women (AAUW) in 1952. She was a co-winner of the Flagstaff Citizen of the Year Award for 1975, the homecoming dedicatee for 1948, and the first faculty member to receive the Gold Axe Award. Agnes Allen served on the National Advisory Council on Health Professions Education in 1975 and received the Conservation Service Award in that same year.

Opposite: Allen Hall (1968) as it opened. Raymond and McDonald Halls and the Field House are in the background.

Below: Allen Hall (2008).

Chemistry Building

The Chemistry Building opened in fall 1968 and was dedicated on the same day as the Biology Building. The name Physical Sciences, lettered on the north side of the building, came about, in part, because a portion of the Department of Geology, then still incorporating Geography, shared the building with Chemistry. The building is exemplary of the International style of architecture with ribbon windows and spandrel panels. In 1985, $550,000 covered the cost for a new set of fume hoods for laboratories and research areas.

The building currently houses portions of the Department of Chemistry and Biochemistry. In the past seven years, major portions of the laboratory instruction and research functions of the department shifted to the Wettaw Building and the New Laboratory Facility. Classroom teaching and most faculty offices remain in the older structure.

The Center for Science Teaching and Learning (CSTL) resides partly in the Chemistry Building. CSTL focuses on development and implementation of new learning techniques and sponsors programs for in-service teachers at Flagstaff and throughout Arizona. Several members of the Department of Biological Sciences have office and laboratory space in the Chemistry Building. In addition to the aforementioned occupancy by the Geology Department, Philosophy was housed in the Chemistry Building for many years, as were members of the Department of Mathematics.

East side of the Chemistry Building (ca. 1970).

View of the east and north sides of the Chemistry Building (2008).

Anthropology Laboratory

The Department of Anthropology initiated an archaeology program in 1976, with space in Hanley Hall. Both units moved to the Social and Behavioral Sciences Building and then to the Bilby Research Center. Today, Anthropology research spaces are in the Emerald City swing space, the Bilby Research Center, and, as of 1989–1990, the former Office of Facilities Development and Construction Services, renamed the Anthropology Laboratory. Contracts with the Bureau of Land Reclamation, the Navajo Nation, the Hopi Tribe, the National Park Service, and other cultural entities provide a strong foundation for research and excellent opportunities for undergraduate and graduate students to gain exposure to modern archaeology.

The building opened in 1977 as the Naval Reserve Building. With the discontinuation of the program in 1978–1979, the NAU Police Department moved into the structure, followed in 1986–1987 by the Office of Facilities Development and Construction Services. The building design is International with the steel support pillars exposed, reflecting the honesty of this style.

There were two mobile units, referred to as Anthropology Annex A and Annex B, located adjacent to the laboratory. They served as the home, from 1992 to 2002, for federally funded studies of HIV prevention. When the grant program ended, the trailers became headquarters for construction of McKay Village and were then demolished.

View of the Anthropology Laboratory (ca. 1980) at the time the Bilby Center was under construction.

The Anthropology Laboratory (2007), with McKay Village in the background.

Reilly Hall

Reilly Hall opened in 1969. Originally referred to as Dorm L, then High Rise #2 and Women's High Rise during planning and construction, this building is in the modern International style, similar to nearby Sechrist Hall, with a symmetrical stone facade. The name became West High Rise Dorm by 1980, and in 1986 ABOR changed it to Reilly Hall. Initially housing 570 female students, the facility is now a coeducational residence hall with 544 students. Reilly Hall features an exercise room, a computer and study room, and a resource center.

Biography

William P. Reilly, born in Oakland, California, in 1908, was an important public service figure in Arizona over many decades. He attended local schools in Nutley, New Jersey, but dropped out of high school. He reentered school and graduated from the U.S. Coast Guard Academy.

Reilly spent most of his professional career in public service. He was an adviser to Governors Wesley Bolin and Bruce Babbitt, and served stints as interim director for state departments of Corrections, Revenue, and Administration. He was president of Arizona Public Service Company, including the period when the Salt River Project began. Reilly was a founder of the Phoenix 40, now the Greater Phoenix Leadership group. He also served as a member of ABOR from 1980 to 1986.

For his many civic and charitable contributions, Reilly received numerous accolades, including a Samaritan Health Service Award. He served on the board of directors for University Medical Center in Tucson, St. Joseph's Hospital in Phoenix, Mercy Health Care System, and the Cactus Pine Girl Scouts. Reilly entered the U.S. Coast Guard Athletic Hall of Fame in 2003, having played both football and baseball during his years at the Academy. In 1986, he received the James Creasman Award of Excellence at the Arizona State University Founders Day ceremonies. Soon before his death from cancer, Reilly was given an honorary degree from the University of Arizona. He died on November 23, 1986, in Phoenix.

William P. Reilly.

Opposite: View of Reilly Hall (1970s).

Reilly Hall (2008).

Performing and Fine Arts Building and Ardrey Auditorium

The Performing and Fine Arts Building and Ardrey Auditorium opened in 1969 and 1972, respectively. The two-phase project featured modern International-style architecture with mansard-like rooflines, which were making a comeback nationally at that time. The first phase of construction, Performing and Fine Arts, was known originally as Creative and Communication Arts. The second phase of the project, the construction of Ardrey Auditorium, finished in 1972.

The Performing and Fine Arts space features offices, classrooms, music practice rooms, choral and instrumental practice rooms, the Beasley Art Museum, the Clifford E. White Theatre (which seats 600), and the Studio Theatre (with seating for 150). There are studios and practice rooms for the NAU student orchestra, several bands, choral groups, and individual voice and instrumental instruction. The two theater venues are home to NAU drama productions, summer theater, and smaller music performances. This facility received $800,000 in renovations over the first twenty-five years. In 1997–1998, both buildings received an extensive $10.3 million renovation, which entailed a new north-south walkway through the complex, new practice rooms, major upgrades in the Clifford White Theatre and Ardrey Auditorium, and additional acoustic insulation.

When it opened, the Creative and Communication Arts Building housed Journalism, an art foundry, and the campus radio station on the first floor; the Art Department, classrooms for humanities, and art galleries and studios resided on the second floor; the third floor contained the Drama Department, theater support facilities, and the small theater. In 1976, a small shed, attached to the rear of the building and referred to as the Sculpture Building, provided space for sculpture and glass blowing. These somewhat hazardous activities had homes in several of the Stone Cottages, across from the stands at Lumberjack Stadium, and in the Plateau Center, prior to occupying the former Recycling Building on South Campus in 2007.

Ardrey Auditorium seats 1,550 people and features a $200,000 Austin pipe organ, installed in 1976. The concert hall provides a home for the Flagstaff Symphony Orchestra, the NAU Orchestra, the Master Chorale of Flagstaff, and numerous other organizations. The hall also hosts guest artists and performances. Since 1980, more than $1.6 million in renovations have included stage modification, addressing safety issues, and numerous smaller changes, such as upgrading the lobby.

One anecdote about the stage in Ardrey Auditorium is worth noting. A desire to stage Wagner's Ring Cycle, a series of four operas, required an orchestra pit large enough to include an area under the main stage. The wall between the existing orchestra pit and the stage was cement. With great care, removal of the wall preceded placement of a large I-beam underneath and extending across the front of the stage. A new orchestra pit could fit both in front of and beneath the stage.

Biographies

Clifford E. White was born on October 1, 1925, in Flint, Michigan. During the Great Depression, the family moved to Detroit where White graduated from Redford High School in 1943. He immediately enlisted in the U.S. Navy, serving in the Medical Corps in the Philippines until conclusion of the Pacific War. He returned to Detroit and obtained bachelor of science, master of science, and doctorate degrees from Wayne State University, in disciplines pertaining to speech and theater. He spent many happy hours singing with a variety of groups, in his home area and in the military, and taught school in the Detroit area and at Wayne State. White was a televised instructor of American literature for Michigan public schools. He was a member of the faculty at NAU for twenty-four years, from 1968 to 1992. He served as chair of the Speech and Theatre Department for many years and helped introduce speech pathology to the NAU curriculum. White involved himself in university and local theater as an actor and director. In 1994, NAU dedicated the Clifford White Theatre to honor his contributions to the arts. His wife, Doris, also heavily involved theater, was the key person in establishing Theatrikos, a local theater company with a strong reputation. Clifford White died on December 26, 2008, at home in Flagstaff.

Clifford White.

Ardrey Auditorium and the bridge to Performing and Fine Arts,
with part of the latter structure visible at the right.

Eldon Ardrey was born on May 24, 1905, in Safford County, Kansas. His early schooling occurred in rural Kansas, followed by a bachelor of arts degree from the University of Kansas in 1928. Ardrey earned his master of science degree from Yankton College (closed in 1984) in South Dakota in 1931, where he taught strings and musical theory. He obtained his doctorate in education from the University of Colorado (at Boulder) in 1959. He first came to Flagstaff and the state college in the summer of 1929 for a musical activity. He and his wife, Ruth, returned in 1931 when Grady Gammage, the school president, asked him to serve as chair of the Department of Music. The couple remained in Flagstaff for the remainder of their lives, including forty-one years on the faculty for Eldon Ardrey. During those four decades, the Music Department moved from the basement of Old Main to portions of the Ashurst Building, which became Ashurst Music Hall with practice rooms, studios, several classrooms, and offices, in addition to the renovated main hall. Near the end of his life, Ardrey witnessed the transition to what was then the Creative and Communication Arts Building.

During his long tenure with the school, Eldon Ardrey accomplished many firsts at the college and within the local community. He founded the Shrine of Ages Choir in 1932, directed it for twenty-five years, and provided the first Easter Sunday Sunrise Services at the Grand Canyon in 1935. The annual event was broadcast live on a national radio network for many decades. Ardrey organized the first Arizona All-State Orchestra in 1939 and conducted the orchestra during the ensuing decades, providing a program that continues today. He was a co-founder of the Flagstaff Festival of the Arts, which used a variety of venues for music, art exhibits, dance, and theater performances, including, in the later years, Ardrey Auditorium. Ardrey served on the Arizona State Commission for the Arts from 1967 to 1970. He also co-founded the NAU Summer Music Camp.

Eldon Ardrey became director of the Liberal Arts Division in 1958 and then the first dean of the College of Creative Arts in 1966. Eldon and Ruth Ardrey were the joint homecoming dedicatees for 1957. His son, Roger, a baritone vocalist, joined the music faculty at NAU for six years. Eldon Ardrey died in Flagstaff on March 6, 1969.

Eldon Ardrey.

The Performing and Fine Arts Building (2008).

A view of Ardrey Auditorium's east facade (2008).

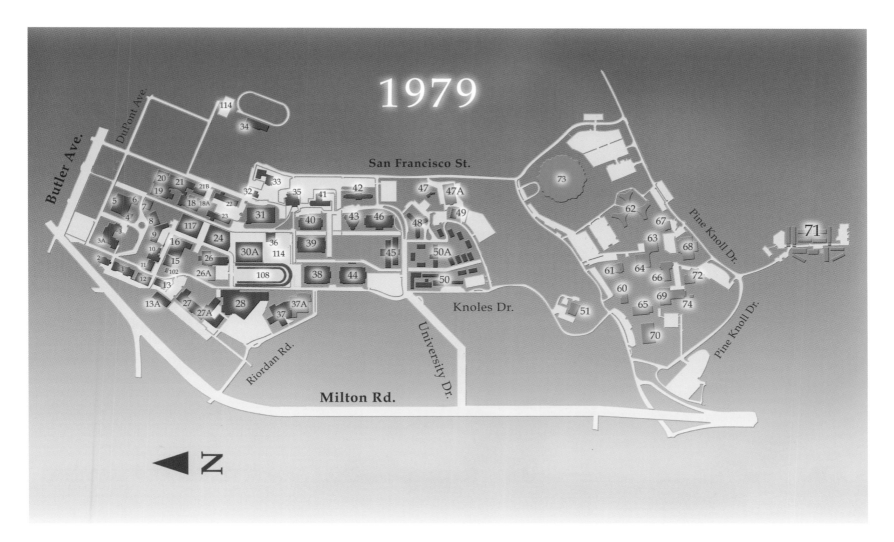

1979

The 1979 map depicts the location of the buildings that existed on campus at the end of the presidency of J. Lawrence Walkup. All buildings highlighted in orange were constructed during the last ten years of the Walkup presidency. Virtually all of this growth reflects the expansion to the South Academic Center, later called the South Campus. This map corresponds to the second half of the text of chapter 3. (Note: No aerial photograph was located for 1979 or any year near that date. (A key for building numbers is on page 301.)

Health Professions Building

The Science Building for the South Academic Center opened in 1970. The concept of a separate campus originated with President Walkup in the late 1960s. The plan was to have the North Academic Center accommodate eight thousand students, with the South Academic Center enrolling approximately four thousand students. The package approved by ABOR in early 1969 for constructing the South Academic Center included allocations for a liberal arts building (today's Social and Behavioral Sciences

The Science Building at the South Academic Center (early 1970s).

Building, $1.4 million), a science building (Health Professions Building, $1.5 million), a dormitory (McConnell Hall, $3.2 million), a heating plant building ($750,000), and a student union (South Union and part of the du Bois Center, $1.0 million). A request in spring 1969 provided an additional $875,000 for a library.

The South Academic Center was self-contained with a College of Scientific and Humanistic Studies and Colleges of Business and Engineering.

The Science Building, later named Health Sciences and then Health Professions, was one of the first structures completed on South Campus. The architectural style is International with features including casement windows, a two-tone facade, and the presence of spandrel panels. The building housed faculty from the humanities and sciences, as well as those affiliated with the health professions. A Department of Physiology and Microbiology provided instruction in fields required for training in the health professions.

The Department of Health Sciences has a wing with offices and classrooms, a 155-seat lecture hall, and a wing with laboratory facilities. In 1978, the Nursing Department acquired its own building, and in 2005, the Exercise Science Program joined the Department of Biological Sciences. In 1983, Speech Pathology (Communication Sciences and Disorders) moved from the Performing and Fine Arts Building to the Health Professions Building. Clinics for dental hygiene, physical therapy, and speech and audiology, located in the Health Professions Building, provide training for students and a service to the local community. Current occupants are the Departments of Dental Hygiene, Rehabilitation Sciences with Athletic Training, Communications Sciences and Disorders, Health Sciences, and Physical Therapy.

The Health Professions Building (2007).

Learning Resources Center

The South Learning Center (Learning Resources Center) opened in 1972 as the Library Study Center and/or South Campus Academic Center. The architecture is similar to the Social and Behavioral Sciences Building and others at the South Academic Center, in the International style with sloping or bannered exterior walls. The architecture of South Campus simultaneously moved beyond Euro-American architecture precedents while honoring pre-Columbian societies of Mexico and Central America with bannered exterior walls.

For a time, the Study Center was a branch of Cline Library and Special Collections and Archives; these holdings moved back to Cline Library in 1992. At present, the Learning Resources Center is an excellent place for study, with computer stations, group study areas, the South Learning Assistance Center, and training workshops covering study skills and time management.

Library Study Center at the South Academic Center (1975).

Learning Resources Center (2007).

Raul Castro Social and Behavioral Sciences Building

As the South Academic Center emerged, one of the earliest structures was the Liberal Arts Building, now Social and Behavioral Sciences (SBS). Between its initial designation in 1972 and its current one, the building bore the names Public and Environmental Service and College of Humanistic and Scientific Studies. SBS has classrooms of varying sizes and a two-hundred-seat auditorium. The architecture is similar to others on South Campus, an Aztec flare with sloping sides, to recognize pre-Colombian Native American societies.

In 1981, the College of Public and Environmental Service, housed in this building, was dissolved and faculty members from the Center for Integrated Studies moved back to their home departments to rejoin colleagues working in the same academic areas. The building's name changed to Social and Behavioral Sciences in 1984.

In 2008, NAU honored the only Latino governor in Arizona history, Raul H. Castro, by naming the Social and Behavioral Sciences Building in his honor. The Departments of Sociology and Social Work, Psychology, Criminal Justice, and portions of Anthropology currently use the building. Political Science and Sociology were originally part of a joint Department of Social Science with History, but moved to the South Academic Center in the early 1970s as a separate unit. Anthropology originated in the Department of Biology and moved, as a separate unit, to the South Academic Center in the early 1970s. Sociology resided in the Liberal Arts and Biology Buildings until it shifted to the South Academic Center.

Criminal Justice, originally called Police Science and then Police Science and Administration, initially occupied space in the Liberal Arts Building. The department moved to the du Bois Center basement and then to its present location in SBS. Some units in this college moved to the west wing of SBS, the former College of Business Administration, including Women's Studies, Ethnic Studies, and the Social Research Laboratory (closed in 2009).

Biography

Raul Hector Castro was born on June 12, 1916, in Cananea, Mexico, the son of a copper miner and midwife. He was the second youngest of fourteen children. He moved to Douglas, Arizona, at age ten. His father died when he was twelve, but despite needing to make his own way in the world, Castro received an honors degree from Douglas High School. Through hard work, Castro saved funds to attend ASTCF, receiving his degree in elementary education in 1939, the same year he attained U.S. citizenship. Jobs held before he attended college included waiting tables in various eating establishments, mining gold, and plucking chickens. At ASTCF, he was captain of both the track and boxing teams, and in 1988 he was elected to the NAU Athletic Hall of Fame.

Denied the chance to teach in Douglas, he left Arizona to work in fruit orchards and wander the West by rail. Castro spent some time as a Foreign Service clerk in Agua Prieta, Mexico (across the border from Douglas). He

Raul Castro.

Opposite: The South Academic Center's Liberal Arts Building (early 1970s).

attended the University of Arizona Law School, graduating in 1949. He practiced law in Pima County, became deputy county attorney, and was elected county attorney and served until 1958. He was a superior court judge from 1958 to 1964, gaining national recognition for his compassion for those who passed through his court.

President Lyndon Johnson nominated him as ambassador to El Salvador in 1964, a position he held until 1968, when he became ambassador to Colombia. In 1969, he returned to Arizona and specialized in international law, including immigration and naturalization. His rise in the Democratic Party in Arizona resulted in nomination for governor in 1970, but he lost in a close race. Nominated again in 1974, he became governor and served until 1977. In 1977, President Carter appointed him ambassador to Argentina. Raul Castro lives today in southern Arizona and continues to practice international law.

Liberal Arts Building as the College of Public and Environmental Service (ca. 1975).

Left: East side of the Raul Castro Social and Behavioral Sciences Building (2008).

Below: Main entrance of the Raul Castro Social and Behavioral Sciences Building (2008).

Heating Plant Annex

Called Central Heating upon completion in 1972, this structure became the Heating Plant Annex in 1976. A new boiler debuted in 1999 at a cost of $316,000. In 2003–2004, the size of the structure doubled to include a chiller system for South Campus. In a familiar architectural pattern on South Campus, the original building is designed in the International style with sloping outer walls, a Native American influence. In 2005 another addition included bannered buttresses and a glass wall on the north side, exposing the interior of the building.

Heating Plant Annex (2008) with the 2003–2004 addition.

The Heating Plant Annex on South Campus (1970s), with a small portion of McConnell Hall in the background.

du Bois Conference Center and South Dining Hall

In 1971, the South Dining Hall and the du Bois Conference Center opened; the two were later connected with an expansion that fit in between. Three different buildings on the NAU campus have had the name South Dining Hall. The first of these became part of the food services wing of the University Union and eventually was called Central Dining. A second structure, now the Gateway Student Success Center, was briefly called South Dining after its completion, but became University Commons. The third structure to be named South Dining is the building covered here.

Construction of the South Dining Hall was finished in 1970. It has a cafeteria, a coffee shop, and "The Peaks"—a food service area, located in the connector between the du Bois Conference Center and the South Dining Hall. A fire in 1970, during construction, caused $80,000 damage, slowing the building's completion. The design is late modern or early postmodern in style, with peaks of the buildings' rooflines matching those of the San Francisco Peaks. Today, as a combined facility, with dining and conferences, this is a lively and dynamic gathering place, with views of mountains and forests.

The du Bois Conference Center has the same style as South Dining. In April 1988, the structure was renamed in honor of Alan van Fleet du Bois, a Phoenix businessman and philanthropist. The building has a large ballroom that seats six hundred, and a series of smaller rooms that accommodate twenty-five to seventy people. Smaller rooms provide meeting space for numerous university committees and campus organizations. The ballroom serves many campus functions, including awards ceremonies, celebrations of

student research accomplishments, and the annual Holiday Choral Dinner. The conference center serves community events such as business development workshops, speaker presentations, summer camps, and United Way celebrations.

In 1991, the connection between the du Bois Center and South Dining Hall opened. In 1994–1995, modifications in the basement provided for classroom and office spaces. Until mid-2007, a key occupant of the basement facilities was the Institute for Tribal Environmental Professionals (ITEP). This unit receives funding from a variety of sources, most notably the Environmental Protection Agency (EPA). ITEP provides advice and training to tribal groups around the country on issues like air quality, groundwater, and community health concerns. Today, ITEP is located in swing space in Peterson Hall.

At an earlier time, Police Science (Criminal Justice) occupied the basement, with a firing range. The "Icicles" sculpture (or "French Fries") on the plaza at the southwest corner of the du Bois Center hides the range's vent system. The range was tested, but never fully used, due to a variety of problems. The Arizona Department of Public Safety used the criminology laboratory and evidence lockers in this basement facility. The criminology laboratory opened with a grant of $470,000 from the state. The facility aided local law enforcement, provided internship opportunities for students interested in law enforcement, and facilitated developments in forensics through research. Over time, the crime lab moved to other locations in Flagstaff. By 2008, laboratories associated with psychology moved to the basement area.

South Dining and the du Bois Conference Center (ca. 1970) near the end of construction.

Biography

Alan van Fleet du Bois was born in Arizona in 1914. He fought in the Pacific Theater as a Marine during World War II and returned with five Purple Hearts, a Bronze Star, and two Silver Stars. When the Japanese struck Pearl Harbor on December 7, 1941, du Bois and some friends were playing golf at Oahu Country Club. He enlisted, trained as a sniper, and continued as an expert shot until late in life.

After the war, du Bois obtained a degree in psychology at Arizona State University. Alan du Bois was a well-known Phoenix philanthropist. Among his contributions is the E. Blois du Bois Foundation Forestry Scholarship at NAU. The foundation, established in 1966, also provides scholarships at the University of Arizona and Arizona State University.

Alan van Fleet du Bois (second from left) congratulating students on the occasion of scholarship awards.

South Dining Hall (2008).

du Bois Conference Center (2008) with the "Icicles" sculpture designed
to hide the venting system for the pistol range in the basement.

McConnell Hall

In early 1969, ABOR approved funding for a dormitory for eight hundred students at the new South Academic Center. McConnell Hall, originally named the South Academic Center Dormitory, then South Campus Hall, and then South Hall, exhibits a modern International style with spandrel panels between the windows. There is a nice contrast between McConnell Hall and the neighboring McKay Village complex, which is neo-Craftsman, a popular postmodern style. McConnell Hall suffered roof problems on several occasions. Many of the buildings at NAU experience roof problems, likely due to the climate, with temperatures dipping below freezing on many nights, followed by warm days. That freeze-thaw cycle takes a toll on structures and particularly the roofs.

McConnell Hall has shared rooms and common bathrooms and is the only traditional residence hall with carpeting. The eight hundred students who live here, in the largest housing unit on campus, are away from any significant road traffic, are surrounded by mature pine trees, and enjoy amenities such as study lounges and a resource room. McConnell Hall is near the Skydome and the South Union, including its dining facility.

Biography

Samuel A. McConnell Jr. was born on January 7, 1924, in El Paso, Texas. He grew up in Indiana, attended local public schools, and received a degree in pharmacology in 1950. He moved to Williams, Arizona, in 1960, where he was a partner in the McCrary-McConnell Pharmacy. He was active in local affairs, serving as president of the Parent-Teacher Association and, later, as president of the Arizona Pharmaceutical Association. He won election to the Arizona State Legislature in 1966 as a Republican from Coconino County and was in his tenth term when he died in Phoenix on July 21, 1986. During his legislative service, he was speaker pro tem and had the distinction of being the longest-serving chair of the Rules Committee. In Flagstaff, McConnell was assistant manager at the new Flagstaff Mall in the 1970s and held memberships in the Kiwanis Club and chamber of commerce. He was a strong supporter of NAU, aiding efforts to obtain funds for the construction that occurred during the 1970s, particularly the South Academic Center.

Samuel A. McConnell.

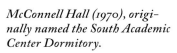

*McConnell Hall (1970), origi-
nally named the South Academic
Center Dormitory.*

*South face of McConnell Hall
(2007) from the same perspective as the 1970 photo.*

Main entrance of McConnell Hall (2007).

Anthropology Building

(No Longer Standing)

The Anthropology Building, demolished in July 2004 to make way for the new Business Administration Building, originally housed the administration for the South Academic Center. The building's style was modern International with the sloping outer walls characteristic of many South Campus buildings. By 1977, with the university administration once again centralized, Computer Services occupied the building with a renovation to accommodate their needs.

Anthropology started on campus in the early 1950s with a single faculty member, Robert C. Euler, who was part of the Biology Department. Beginning in the mid-1960s, the program acquired its own identity and underwent a period of growth. When the South Academic Center opened in 1970–1971, Anthropology was part of the new College of Scientific and Humanistic Studies. In 1981, the Department of Anthropology joined with Psychology, Political Science, Geography, and Sociology to form the College of Social and Behavioral Sciences.

In 1989, the Department of Anthropology moved to its own building, the former Administration Building and Computer Center, where, for a time, it shared space with the Department of Geography. With demolition of this structure, the Anthropology Department moved to Emerald City, with additional space in the Social and Behavioral Sciences Building, Bilby Research Center, and Anthropology Laboratory.

The Administration Building for the South Academic Center (ca. 1975).

Anthropology Building (2003) just prior to demolition to make way for a new
Business Administration Building. (Photo courtesy of Robert Trotter.)

Engineering and Technology Building

By the mid-1960s, what started as Industrial and Manual Arts grew with the needs of the state and country. In 1967, ABOR gave approval for NAU to grant a bachelor of science in engineering. The College of Engineering and Technology featured four areas: civil engineering, electronics, mechanical engineering, and drafting. The college moved from the Communications Building to a new structure built at the South Academic Center. This facility, featuring a modern International architectural style with ribbon windows, opened in 1972.

By the late 1980s, the areas of study in the College of Engineering and Technology consisted of computer science, engineering (civil, electrical, and environmental), and engineering technology. The last of these involves applications of various aspects of engineering to practical problems such as drafting and electronics. Still further change is evident with the 1995 addition of a program in construction management. In 2008, there were separate bachelor's degrees in civil engineering, environmental engineering, computer science and engineering, construction management, electrical engineering, and mechanical engineering.

At the start of the new millennium, expanded and modern facilities were needed to accommodate changes in the engineering curriculum. A major project to meet these needs—involving a sleek-looking postmodern facade emphasizing glass, smooth surfaces, and trapezoidal rooflines—changed the entire face of the building. A portion of the original architecture remains on the south end of the structure, providing a unique contrast of styles. This major renovation was dedicated on April 11, 2006.

Engineering and Technology Building (early 1970s).

*The Engineering Building after the 2003 remodel and addition,
showing some of the original building to the left rear.*

Current Engineering Building (2008) with the north-facing
glass facade reflecting the surrounding trees and buildings.

Rolle Activity Center

Built as the South Activity Center in 1972, dedicated on October 23, 1973, and renamed for Joseph C. Rolle in 1989, this facility serves at least three functions. It hosts Intramurals and Recreation, Physical Education, and Intercollegiate Athletics, including volleyball and some basketball. NAU uses the main court area for various ceremonies and campus functions. Bleachers provide seating for nearly 1,100 people for sporting events. The structure features a modern International style with bannered buttresses and sloping outer walls, a Native American–Aztec reference characteristic of South Campus architecture. The building houses locker rooms, courts for activities, offices, and classrooms. When the structure opened, it was immediately evident that a plumbing mix-up had occurred. In the men's locker room, the urinals flushed with hot water and only cold water was available for showers.

Biography

Joseph C. Rolle was born on September 5, 1917, in Bisbee, Arizona. After early schooling in his hometown, Rolle received his bachelor of arts (1941) and his master of arts (1950) in education from ASCF. He played basketball all four years in college, was captain of the team as a senior, and was on the football and track teams. He was president of the Associated Students for the academic years 1939–1940 and 1940–1941 and received the President's Prize in 1940. Rolle paid for much of his college education by working in the dining hall; Mother Hanley was his supervisor, mentor, and lifelong friend. He later obtained a professional diploma in education from the Teachers College at Columbia University in 1958. Joe and Marie Rolle were married on December 26, 1941.

From 1942 to 1946, during World War II, Rolle attended Officer Training School in Lexington, Virginia (home of the Virginia Military Institute), and then served twenty months overseas working with occupation troops in the Pacific Theater. Immediately after the war, he worked with the Arizona Tax Commission and then joined the college as an assistant accountant in the business office. When they returned to Flagstaff from Phoenix, the Rolles were proud owners of a Model A Ford. Rolle was frequently asked to loan the car to others and he did, but with two rules. First, the borrower was responsible for putting gas in the car. Second, the borrower needed to fill the radiator with water, and during winter months the responsible person was required to drain that water so it would not freeze.

Beginning in 1947, Rolle became a fixture on the NAU campus, serving in numerous capacities until his retirement in 1982. Most of his positions put him in close contact with students and he assisted many student organizations throughout his career. His positions included bookstore manager and men's dormitory head resident (1947–1953), College Union director (1953–1955), dean of men (1955–1959), dean of students (1959–1969), and dean of University Services (1969–1982).

Joseph C. Rolle received an honorary doctor of humane letters from his alma mater in 1980 and was the NAU homecoming dedicatee in 1956. Together, Joe and Marie Rolle exemplify what it means to be an enduring and valuable part of the NAU and Flagstaff communities. The Joseph C. and Marie Rolle Scholarship Award for Excellence is given each year in their honor.

Joseph C. Rolle.

North entrance of the Rolle Activity Center (2008).

Social and Behavioral Sciences West

The College of Business Administration (CBA) moved from the Adel Building to South Campus in 1973. The opening of the new CBA Building at the South Academic Center was delayed several months owing to the record snowfall during the winter of 1972–1973, which featured the notorious 93-inch storm at the end of the winter holidays. Social and Behavioral Sciences (SBS) West served as home for the CBA for just over thirty years, until 2006, when the college moved to the W. A. Franke Building.

More than $2.8 million in renovations between 1973 and 2005 included remodeling the old Hotel and Restaurant Management spaces, stabilizing the building due to shifting and sinking, infrastructure repairs and improvements, and general refurbishment over time. SBS West has a late modern architectural style, transitioning to postmodern.

The building has units including Ethnic Studies, Applied Indigenous Studies, Geography, Planning and Recreation, Women's Studies, and offices associated with college operations, and its auditorium is named for the ninth president of the college, Tom Bellwood.

Biography

The auditorium in SBS West bears the name of Tom Octavius Bellwood, who served as president of ASCF from 1945 to 1947. Bellwood was born on June 6, 1896, in Heighington, England. His family moved to Central City, Colorado, in 1909 when Tom was twelve, where he graduated from high school in 1915. He worked in his father's cabinet-making shop and at an ore-crushing mill, followed by a year at Barnes Commercial School in Denver. He matriculated to Colorado State Teachers College at Greeley (Northern Colorado University), from which he received his bachelor of arts degree in 1921 and, the following year, his master's

degree in education. While studying for his master's, Bellwood served as assistant pastor for a local Presbyterian church. During his studies, he was secretary to the college dean and registrar from 1918 to 1921.

Bellwood joined the faculty of NANS in 1922 as an instructor in commerce and served as dean of the new College of Business Administration. He became acting president of ASTCF during the academic year 1943–1944 and then president in 1945 upon Thomas Tormey's resignation. Bellwood remained president of the college until 1947, when he stepped down for health reasons. During Bellwood's presidency, the postwar boom in enrollment began and new academic programs were offered for veterans. In 1945, Arizona State Teachers College at Flagstaff received authorization to grant bachelor's degrees in subjects other than education and became Arizona State College at Flagstaff.

After stepping down from the presidency, Bellwood again became dean of the College of Business Administration, returned to the classroom in 1955, and taught until retirement in 1963, at which time he moved to Sedona. Bellwood was the homecoming dedicatee for 1953, which was a fitting tribute because he led the planning for the very first homecoming at the school in 1924.

Tom Bellwood and his wife, Grace, were active members of the Flagstaff community. Bellwood directed the choir at the Federated Community Church and was a member of the church board. He enjoyed riding his motorcycle, something that was relatively new in those days. He received an honorary doctorate from Colorado State Teachers College in 1945. Each year, a student in the College of Business Administration receives a scholarship bearing his name. He died in Flagstaff on August 7, 1971.

Thomas O. Bellwood, ninth president of NAU.

Opposite: Social and Behavioral Sciences West (2008).

View of the east facade of SBS West (2008).

ROTC/Property Control Building

Constructed in 1973 as the Transportation Services (Garage Annex) facility, this structure continues to serve the university in a variety of ways. One of its initial functions included being the training location for the automotive repair education program. In 1989, with the completion of the Capital Assets and Services Building, Facilities Development and Construction Services joined with Property Control and occupied the former Transportation Services Building and the building was renamed Facilities Development.

In 1997, the Air Force ROTC program (aerospace studies) and Army ROTC program (military science) left quarters in the Engineering and Technology Building and the basement of the du Bois Center, respectively, and joined the building's occupants, and Facilities Development shifted to the new structure at the southern end of campus. In 2004, Purchasing Services moved to this building. Surplus Property is housed in the west end of the building.

The west entrance of the ROTC/Property Control Building (2007).

Anechoic Chamber

The smallest stand-alone structure on campus is the Anechoic Chamber, located between the Southwest Forest Science Complex, the Engineering Building, and the Nursing Building. Built in 1972, this facility served for acoustical testing in the absence of any echoes. Thick foam pads on the walls provided anechoic conditions. Another room was used, in connection with solar panels on the ground and roof, to investigate aspects of solar energy production and storage—hence the moniker "Solar Shack." Today, it is a facility to engage students in studies of solar and wind power, and for storage.

Anechoic Chamber and weather instrumentation (2008).

South Family Apartments

As part of the South Academic Center, 152 units for married student and family housing, arranged in thirteen buildings, opened in 1971. Designed in a functional late modern architectural style, each apartment has two bedrooms.

There are both a Community Development Association and a South Family Blockwatch Program. These partially furnished apartments with utilities included, and situated in the ponderosa pines, rented for $629–$747 a month in 2008.

South Family Apartments (2008).

Counseling and Testing Center

This structure was a laboratory facility for Psychology beginning in 1975. It is designed in the modern International style, with soldier courses of brick beneath the windows. When Psychology moved to the South Academic Center in 1972, the Counseling and Testing Center moved to the building that formerly housed the animal quarters—after significant renovations.

Counseling services were available on campus beginning at least as early as the 1960s—first in the form of a psychologist located in the Gammage Building and then through Rehabilitation Services in Eastburn Annex (Institute for Human Development). As the services grew, Counseling and Testing offices moved to the Herrington

House. In 1979, the unit moved to mobile structures situated northeast of the Fronske Student Health Center, and in 1988 it relocated to its present location. Disability Resources and portions of Student Support Services also occupied the building.

The Counseling Center provides professional services for individuals, couples, and groups with psychological concerns. The unit helps to educate NAU students about substance abuse, adjusting to college, and time and stress management. The testing portion of the center's mission provides opportunities for students to take tests for admissions to various levels of education, including colleges, graduate programs, and professional schools.

Counseling and Testing Center (2008).

Babbitt Administrative Center

Called the Executive Center when it opened in 1976, this building became the John G. Babbitt Administrative Center on December 2, 1988. Constructed in a late modern architecture style, the building fits into the surrounding environmental context with bricks of varying colors, ribbon windows, and a functional three-tone facade, including dark windows. As portions of the building transitioned in terms of function and occupants, a total of $1.8 million covered the costs of remodeling and refurbishment over the past thirty years.

In its early years, the Executive Center was home for the major administrative offices that had been located in Gammage. A number of other university functions, including the Alumni Office, Student Affairs, the Office of Grants and Contracts Administration, the NAU Foundation, and University Relations, have called this building home.

Currently, offices located in the Babbitt Administrative Center include the university president, provost, executive vice president and vice presidents for Administration and Finance, Enrollment Management, and University Advancement. Other units located in this building are University Legal Counsel, University Marketing and Public Relations, and offices for special assistants that advise the university administration on topics such as ethnic diversity and relations with the Flagstaff community.

At NAU, unlike a number of campuses, there is no monolithic administration building or complex housing all of the functions associated with running the institution. Instead, the Babbitt Administrative Center is a central focus, with at least six other locations on campus where daily business is conducted. These range from the offices of the registrar and bursar located in the Gammage Building to Purchasing and Property Control in the ROTC/Property Control Building.

The woodland area east of the building, connecting the North and South Academic Centers, was known as Entwood Park. A planned bicycle path was eventually completed. The related plans for benches and even a cross-country ski trail never materialized. However, many older alumni remember using the hill for skiing and "tubing" on the snow.

Biography

John George Babbitt was born on May 19, 1908, in Flagstaff. His father, Charles Babbitt, was one of five Babbitt brothers who came to Arizona from Cincinnati, Ohio, and his mother, Mary Verkamp Babbitt, was from another northern Arizona pioneer family. When he was quite young, the family moved to Los Angeles. Upon completing high school, Babbitt attended Santa Clara University in California (1925–1926) and Georgetown University in Washington, D.C. (1926–1928), and eventually earned his bachelor's degree from Loyola University in Los Angeles in 1929, as class valedictorian. He completed studies at Babson School of Business (Babson College) near Boston, Massachusetts, in 1931 and returned to Flagstaff to work in the family businesses.

John G. Babbitt enjoyed a long and productive career as a businessman and politician. He served as chair of Babbitt Brothers Trading Company and as president and manager of Babbitt Ranches. In 1950–1951, he was president of the Arizona Cattle Growers Association, and in 1952 served as chair of the Arizona section of the American Society of Range Management. In politics, he served on the Flagstaff City Council; in the Arizona State Senate, where he was president from 1948 to 1949; and as a member of the governor's Tax Study Committee. He served two terms on

John G. Babbitt.

ABOR and was twice president of that body. Locally, he served as president of the Flagstaff Rotary Club, as president of the board of trustees for the Flagstaff Community Hospital, and as a director for several banks.

For his many contributions to society, John G. Babbitt garnered a number of accolades and awards. Among these were honorary degrees from the University of Arizona (1965) and Northern Arizona University (1966). Georgetown University presented him in 1969 with the John Carroll Award as a distinguished alumnus. He was Northern Arizona Outstanding Citizen for 1961 and was elected posthumously to the Arizona Business Hall of Fame. In 1964, Pope Paul VI granted him membership in the Knights of Malta. John G. Babbitt died on August 5, 1993, in Flagstaff. His casket traveled from the church to the cemetery on a horse-drawn wagon, honoring his years in ranching.

Babbitt Administrative Center (2008), looking southeast.

J. Lawrence Walkup Skydome

With heavy snows in 1973 and impending athletics needs, plans for a modest ice rink facility mushroomed into a facility called the Ensphere. Ground was broken on September 4, 1975, for a multipurpose complex and indoor stadium. The Ensphere opened in 1977 as the second-largest laminated wood beam structure in the world; only the Astrodome in Houston was larger. Maridan Construction was the primary builder, but other firms contributed to the project. Western Wood Structures of Portland, Oregon, designed the roof and Unadilla Laminated Products from New York fabricated the wooden beams. The building became the Multi Dome Facility for a time and then the J. Lawrence Walkup Skydome, at the 1979 University Honors Convocation, as President Walkup was finishing his term as president.

On September 17, 1977, the first activity in the dome, a football game against the University of Montana, resulted in a victory for NAU.

Bob Hope was to be the featured entertainer for the grand opening. Sadly, Bing Crosby, Hope's partner in many movies, died that week in October 1977. Hope called a good friend, Bill Cosby, who came to Flagstaff to perform in his stead. Hope appeared in October the following year. Others who were featured at the Walkup Skydome include Johnny Cash, Hank Williams Jr., Willie Nelson, Kenny Rogers, Jesse Jackson, ZZ Top, Roy Clark, and the Royal Lipizzaners horse troupe.

Financing for the dome involved public and private resources. Land was courtesy of the Arizona Lumber and Timber Company. Funds from local accounts on campus and fees paid by the students through the Associated Students at Northern Arizona University (ASNAU) were part of the package. The state, however, was the major financial contributor, providing at least $6.5 million of the total cost of more than $8 million.

The Skydome hosts an array of events, at regional and statewide levels. NAU athletic contests use the Skydome, including men's football, women's and men's basketball, and women's and men's track and field. Originally, there was a hockey rink, but it did not last long. By 1980, cracks developed, and the rink was abandoned in late 1985. The Skydome is used for NAU commencement exercises. The dome also serves for student, staff, and faculty recreation.

Regionally and statewide, the dome hosts high school sports, championships for high schools, university conference meets, the Phoenix Cardinals football team's preseason preparations, and, on several occasions, the Phoenix Suns basketball team. The annual Flagstaff Home Show and other community events often use the dome's abundant internal space and ample parking.

A few facts and figures about the Skydome: The regular seating capacity is 15,000, with a possible additional 1,230 people around the arena floor. The diameter of the structure is 502 feet, with a ceiling height at the center of 142 feet. The main floor activity area encompasses 97,000 square feet, the equivalent of 2.2 acres. There are 132 doors around the dome's perimeter. The roof required 1.5 million board feet of southern yellow pine.

The Walkup Skydome received $9.5 million for replacements, renovations, and remodels to keep the structure in good functional and safe operating condition. Nearly every surface in or on the dome has been replaced, including the turf on the arena floor, several significant repairs to the roof coating, and replacement of the track surface. The arena floor has been replaced four times, most recently in spring 2008. For the 2002 turf replacement, Astroturf was purchased that formerly was from Tropicana Field, home of the Tampa Bay Devil Rays baseball team.

View of the Walkup Skydome (1977) shortly after its completion.

Walkup Skydome (2008) looking south from near the Atmospheric Research Observatory.

Biography

J. Lawrence (Larry) Walkup was born on February 26, 1914, in Wheeling, Missouri. His father was a farmer and cattleman. Walkup grew up in this rural setting and completed high school in 1932. He earned his bachelor of science and bachelor of art degrees in 1936 from Central Missouri State College (University at Warrensburg) with majors in science and education. He taught public school in Sheridan, Missouri, near St. Joseph, and became superintendent of schools there. He obtained his master of science degree in science education at the University of Missouri in 1941. He joined the U.S. Navy during World War II, assisting with the training of cadets.

When the war ended, Walkup enrolled in the graduate program for educational administration at the University of Missouri, completing his doctorate in 1948. In June of that year he joined the faculty at ASC in Flagstaff. He became department chair and director of Teacher Placement in 1950, dean of instruction in 1951, and dean of the college in 1955. On October 1, 1957, with President Eastburn on a leave of absence, Walkup became interim president; this became permanent in December 1957. He remained president for twenty-two years, retiring in 1979.

During the Walkup era, significant physical and organizational developments occurred at NAU. The School of Forestry opened in 1959. Arizona State College attained university status in 1966. Walkup's presidency saw the largest physical expansion in school history. Student enrollment grew from 1,691 to 11,301 during his tenure and faculty numbers increased fivefold over these twenty-two years.

One anecdote concerning Walkup relates to his driving skills—people still remember the time he backed into the automobile of a faculty member. It was well known that people wished to avoid traveling to meetings, in Phoenix and elsewhere, if Walkup was driving. He also attained special status for his driving tours of the campus when hosting a prospective faculty hire.

Walkup participated in many activities beyond the university. He was a member of the first board of directors for the Raymond Foundation and served on other boards in Flagstaff, including the First Baptist Church, the Flagstaff Chamber of Commerce, and the Kiwanis Club. In 1950, he was state chair of the Kellogg Foundation Education Program. He was president of the American Association for College Teachers of Education in 1969–1970. For his strong support of the local community, Walkup was Flagstaff Citizen of the Year in 1966.

Walkup wrote two volumes about his years at NAU: *Pride, Promise and Progress: The Development of Northern Arizona University* and "Voices of the Campus: A Supplement to the History of Northern Arizona University, 1946–1979."

In 1943, Larry Walkup and Lucy Meloy, an English and music teacher, were married in Missouri. Their marriage of fifty-nine years was important to the many good things that Walkup accomplished. Lucy Walkup contributed immensely to the efforts of her husband, to the campus community, and to the City of Flagstaff. She remains a warm and graceful figure in the local community.

A distinguished professorship in science education bears Walkup's name, reflecting his strong interest in this important intersection of disciplines. He received the Outstanding Alumni Award from Central Missouri State University and the Faculty-Alumni Gold Medal from the University of Missouri. As he retired in 1979, ABOR recognized his service with the Regents' Medal. J. Lawrence Walkup died on August 7, 2002, at eighty-eight years of age.

J. Lawrence Walkup at about the time (1979) he completed his twenty-two years as president of NAU.

Nursing Sciences Building

233

The Nursing Sciences Building, opened in 1978, is in a transitional late modern, early postmodern style; it resembles the Babbitt Administrative Center. Characteristic features include the use of bricks of different colors, ribbon windows, and a functional three-tone facade. Faculty offices, classrooms, and laboratories are all part of the program for training nurses. Much of the clinical training occurs in hospitals and health facilities in Flagstaff, northern Arizona, and the Phoenix metropolitan area. Additional nursing courses and clinical training take place at facilities in the Navajo Nation, in Tucson, and at NAU in Yuma. The Nursing Building has an Interactive Instructional Television (IITV) classroom.

Entrance to the Nursing Sciences Building (2008).

Moller Center

In 1968, Mr. and Mrs. Joseph A. Moller of Scottsdale donated three acres and two large log structures to the NAU Foundation. Joseph Moller married Dorothy Donnelley, a widow who had, with her husband, constructed the buildings. Moller was a retired, highly decorated U.S. Air Force officer. The first structure built was the lodge and then the house. During a portion of the time that NAU owned the buildings, a caretaker lived on the premises.

The center hosted small conferences, seminars, retreats, and continuing education programs, initially for the College of Business Administration and soon for other units on campus. At times, people attending seminars or workshops stayed in rooms at the nearby Pinewood Country Club. NAU sold the property to Bruce Mill in the late 1980s, in part because costly maintenance made it difficult to retain the buildings. Another factor was that the country club ceased to accept guests from the Moller Center.

Moller Center, located in Munds Park (ca. 1980).

THE MATURATION OF
NORTHERN ARIZONA UNIVERSITY

After significant additions to the university's physical plant during the Walkup years, one might think the campus was complete, or nearly so. However, during the ensuing fourteen years, under the leadership of Eugene Hughes, further building occurred. Moreover, and not readily visible or appreciated, the underground infrastructure was expanded, including increased capacity for electrical consumption, the revised roadway and parking plan, and underground tunnels carrying steam, water, and utilities.

Buildings added during this period varied in terms of function; an eclectic mix of facilities for academics, athletics, physical plant operations, and student residences filled gaps in the physical plant. For example, after closure of the swimming pool in the Riles Building, a new aquatic center opened in 1983. The need for facilities to support research led to completion of the Bilby Center and Greenhouse Complex. As enrollment increased, two residence halls, Gabaldon and Mountain View, provided additional housing for students. The need for expanded campus services was the impetus for a complex of structures for physical plant operations and facilities for information technologies. Student activity fees provided primary funding for the Recreation Center, combining in one location various activities from around campus.

FOUR

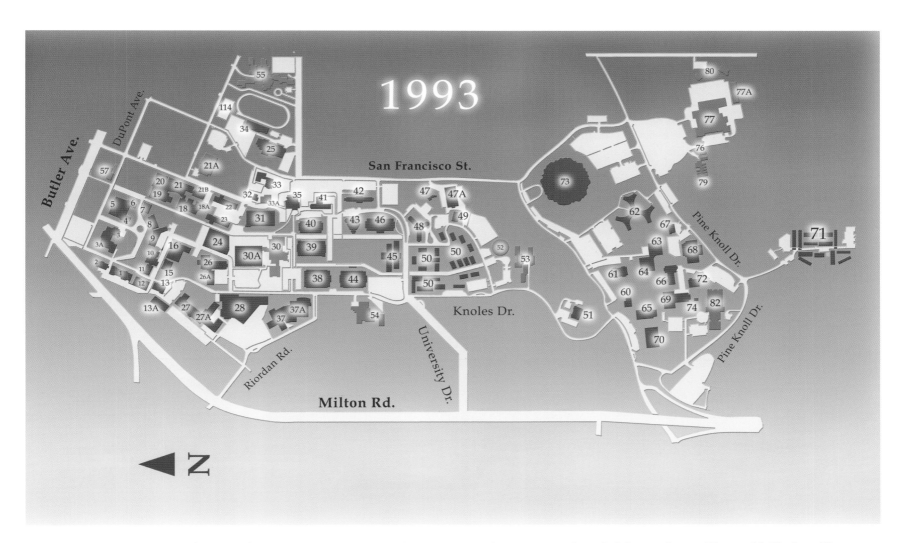

The map and aerial photograph (both 1993) depict the location of the buildings that existed on campus at the end of the presidency of Eugene M. Hughes. All buildings highlighted in orange were constructed during the Hughes presidency. The map corresponds to chapter 4 of the text. Various buildings were added, filling particular needs and with placements that are scattered across the campus. (A key for building numbers is on page 301.)

Fountaine House

Fountaine House (2008), located east of the Mountain View Hall parking garage, serves as a residence for various university staff.

In 1991, the university acquired a house at 631 South Fountaine Street. Fountaine House, built in 1940, is just east of Mountain View Hall and serves as apartments and a single-family residence. Architecturally, it is a raised ranch form, with exaggerated multiple rooflines and a fan light above the front door, indicating later, postmodern influence.

Employee Assistance and Wellness House

The university acquired a private residence at 415 South Beaver Street from the Lopez family in 1947. It is in the Craftsman Bungalow style; a porch at the front of the structure was removed. This location housed the Honors Program and then became home for Employee Assistance and Wellness (EAW) in 1993. The EAW features programs for faculty and staff in areas of physical and mental health and offers counseling services to all NAU employees.

The Employee Assistance and Wellness House (2008), a former private residence on the west side of Beaver Street, houses counselors to assist faculty and staff.

Bilby Research Center

The concept for a research center originated in the late 1970s as NAU developed research capacity in the sciences and related areas. Dedicated in 1981, the Ralph Bilby Research Center opened in 1982. The structure is a mini-dome, mirroring some aspects of the Walkup Skydome, a short distance south. The design is modernist with little ornamentation or features aside from its shape. It has an open-air feeling inside, with high ceilings and movable walls, permitting different configurations for changing needs.

The Bilby Center's mission is to support and encourage original research by NAU faculty. A variety of departments, individually and in cross-disciplinary groups, use the facility and its resources. Research endeavors include paleontology, ecology, archaeology, anthropology, terrestrial ecology, forest entomology, geoscience, and ethnoecology. The Navajo National Archaeology Project was an early occupant of the Bilby Center, and remains to this day. Current resources include scientific illustration and audiovisual services, chemical analysis facilities, and manuscript preparation assistance. Spin-offs from Bilby Center operations include the Avian Cognition Laboratory, Animal Annex, and Greenhouse Complex.

After it opened, the center housed several animal species—not always in their assigned living quarters. Wood rats and pinyon jays, used in ecological and behavioral research, sometimes escaped. Nets prevented birds from damaging equipment and projects. Often at night, staff received calls when liberated wood rats triggered the alarm system. The need for alarms arose due to valuable materials housed within the Navajo Nation Archaeology Project. Scholars and administrators felt relief when the animals found new quarters.

Biography

Ralph Mansfield Bilby was born on June 18, 1917, in Tucson and died on April 1, 1981, in Flagstaff, soon after dedication of the building that bears his name. He attended local schools in Tucson and completed his bachelor of arts at the University of Arizona. He married Mary Eleanor Babbitt in 1941 and entered World War II as a major in the Army Air Corps. Returning to civilian life, he and his wife moved to Flagstaff, where Bilby joined Babbitt Brothers Trading Company, becoming president in 1975. In 1978, he became board chair for the Arizona Public Service Company, a position he held until just prior to his death. Bilby joined ABOR in 1974, serving for six years, including a term as president. Throughout his career, and particularly as a member of ABOR, he was a tireless and tenacious supporter of higher education in Arizona and of NAU.

Ralph Bilby was a substantial presence in local and regional public service, enjoying a term as president of the Flagstaff Chamber of Commerce and as head of the local Republican Party. He served as president of the Arizona Town Hall, an organization that sponsors meetings to discuss issues of importance to Arizona. He was Flagstaff Citizen of the Year in 1973. At the December 1981 commencement, Bilby received an honorary degree. An endowed professorship in the W. A. Franke College of Business and a scholarship honor Ralph Bilby.

Ralph M. Bilby, regent and longtime NAU supporter.

The Bilby Research Center (2008) houses programs and facilities of a cross-disciplinary or integrative nature.

Wall Aquatic Center

Wall Aquatic Center, originally the Natatorium, opened in 1983. The concept for an aquatics facility emerged in the late 1970s; ABOR approved $4.4 million for a natatorium in September 1981. The student activity fee (then $100 per year) partially covered construction costs. It is a very functional structure in the modern International style. The building contains a 50-meter swimming pool and diving complex, a small weight room, offices for coaches and staff, and a lap pool. The main pool holds 704,000 gallons, the diving tank has four diving boards, and a gallery seats 350 spectators. The facility was part of the U.S. Olympic Committee designated training site at NAU, associated with the High Altitude Training Center. Renovations in 1996 added 25-meter lap lanes at a cost of $2.4 million.

Biography

Douglas J. Wall was born on April 1, 1927, in Denver, Colorado. He grew up in Colorado and Kansas, graduated from Kemper Military School (Booneville, Missouri), and served in the U.S. Navy at the conclusion of World War II. He received both bachelor of science (1951) and juris doctor (1955) degrees from the University of Kansas. During his final two years of law school, he was a swimming coach.

Wall passed the Arizona bar exam in 1956 and began law practice, working initially for Valley National Bank in Phoenix and then Flagstaff. From 1959 to 1988, he was a partner in the Flagstaff law firm of Magnum, Wall, Stoops, and Warden. Concurrently he was, from 1963 to 1983, a lecturer for business law at NAU.

Doug Wall provided outstanding service at the local, state, and national levels. Locally, he was a trustee of the Museum of Northern Arizona, the Arizona Community Foundation, and Embry-Riddle University. In Flagstaff, he was a member of the board of directors for numerous organizations, including the Flagstaff Chamber of Commerce, Arizona Public Service, Babbitt Brothers Trading Company, and Northern Arizona Healthcare Foundation. He served as chair of the Arizona Water Commission from 1965 to 1969. Governor Evan Mecham appointed Wall to ABOR in 1988 for an eight-year term. He is on the board of trustees at the University Medical Center Corporation in Tucson and served as chair beginning in 2005. He is a board member of the Arizona Hospital Association, the Committee on Governance of the American Hospital Association, and the Regional Policy Board for the Rocky Mountain States.

Wall practiced law in areas of probate and estate planning, real estate, corporations, and partnerships and was legal counsel for NAU from 1963 to 1983. In May 1996, Doug Wall received an honorary degree and the Natatorium was renamed the Douglas Wall Aquatic Center.

Douglas J. Wall, longtime legal counsel for the university and a prominent Flagstaff lawyer.

Wall Aquatic Center (2008) houses facilities for swimming, diving, and other aquatic activities.

Gabaldon Hall

Gabaldon Hall, originally the Ridge, opened in 1998, houses six hundred students, and sits in the south-central portion of campus. One of the three largest residence halls, its design is early postmodern, with one stone belt course and multiple colors of stonework.

Gabaldon Hall has a suite-style interior configuration and is coeducational, housing mostly upper-class students. Given its amenities and location, Gabaldon Hall has hosted many summer workshops and conferences. The large lawn south of Gabaldon serves many activities including sports, sunbathing, and studying on warm fall and spring days.

Anthony Gabaldon (left) in a classroom with students. He was an outstanding educator and served northern Arizona at the state legislature for many years.

Biography

Anthony (Tony) Gabaldon was born on June 30, 1930, in Belen, New Mexico. He moved to Flagstaff in 1943, where he lived with an older brother. He graduated from Flagstaff High School in 1949 and was All-State quarterback in football that school year. Gabaldon received his bachelor of science (1953) and master of science (1957) degrees in education from NAU. As an undergraduate, he worked at the Black Bat Café, where he was a first-rate chef. He taught at Marshall Elementary School in town and became the first principal of the new Sechrist Elementary School in 1962. At Sechrist, Gabaldon began having sixth-grade students spend a week at Camp Colton at the base of the San Francisco Peaks, enjoying a firsthand environmental education. This program continues today, some forty years after inception.

Gabaldon won election to the Arizona State Senate in 1972 and served eight terms. For four years, he chaired the Senate Committee on Education. He was a co-sponsor of legislation granting authority to build the Walkup Skydome. At a time when the building boom was in full swing at NAU, Tony Gabaldon was its champion in the legislature.

He returned to local politics in 1992, winning election to the Coconino County Board of Supervisors. He was a member of the board for the NAU Foundation, and became the first director of Northern Arizona Head Start (a volunteer position). Among his children is Diana Gabaldon, a best-selling author, NAU graduate with a bachelor of science (zoology) and a doctorate (ecology), and honorary NAU degree recipient in 2007. Anthony Gabaldon died on January 3, 1998, in Phoenix.

Opposite: The large, multi-building residence named the Ridge (1984) is nestled in the ponderosa pines on Central Campus.

Gabaldon Hall (2008), with the open field to the south.

Information Technology Services Building and Annex

Information Technology Services (ITS) occupies two interconnected structures of similar styles and a smaller annex. In 1986, all computer services and related infrastructure moved from the former administration building on South Campus to this new complex on Central Campus. Additions in 1989 and 1996 provided expansion space. Here, NAU maintains the staff and equipment to support computer and telecommunications systems. Other ITS operations are located in Bury Hall on North Campus. The building has a modernist design, characterized by red panels and roofs that contrast sharply with the many surrounding ponderosa pines. As information technology increased through the 1980s and 1990s, ITS staff grew from 17 in 1977 to about 60 in 1990; today there are approximately 120 employees, housed in three locations on campus.

Constructed in several stages, the Information Technology Services complex is home for the computer technologies on campus as well as telecommunications and related services.

Capital Assets and Services Building and Annex

Over the first seventy years, physical plant operations occupied various scattered locations on campus. By the 1970s, some functions were in separate structures like the Transportation Services and Facilities Development Buildings, while others resided in the Plateau Center. In 1984, a plan developed to combine physical plant operations and equipment at the County Yard at the southwest corner of campus, near Interstate 17. Instead, NAU built a new structure.

The university built two structures on the hill at the southeast corner of campus in 1988 and 1989, respectively. The larger structure features a modern-style front with

Front view of the Capital Assets and Services Building.

ribbon windows and side and rear portions of purely functional metal-sided walls. The building has a spacious interior with flexibility for easy renovation as needs change. Located here are the trades, including electrical, paint, fire life safety, HVAC, custodial, grounds, environmental health and safety, lock shop, planning and development, and administration. Views from the front of the building north to the San Francisco Peaks are superb.

Behind the main building is the Capital Assets and Services Annex, occupied by Transportation Services and used as storage for vehicles and equipment.

The Capital Assets and Services Annex houses vehicles and other motorized equipment used to maintain the campus. Note the gas pumps and the many bays on the garage building.

Avian Cognition Laboratory

The Avian Cognition Laboratory opened in 1988. The complex of indoor and outdoor aviaries and a series of testing rooms are for studying bird processes involved in storing and relocating buried seeds. This field of investigation, termed avian cognition, is of interest to scholars of ecology, behavior, learning, and neurobiology because of insights obtained through careful exploration of information storage and retrieval capacities of the pinyon jays and other birds. The architecture is purely functional, a metal-sided shed or barn with interesting cantilevering on the sides.

Greenhouse Complex

The Greenhouse Complex is a research facility and, occasionally, a nursery for campus landscaping and production of tree seedlings for reforestation. There are three large greenhouses and a building for laboratory work, management, and control. The L-shaped building is architecturally interesting in terms of the pillars on the ends of the front and a roofline suggesting some postmodern influences. Built in 1989 and expanded in 1992, funding for the complex came from an NAU administration match of a National Science Foundation grant. With an elevation of 7,000 feet and the control systems in the greenhouses, it is possible to produce conditions representative of climates ranging from desert to alpine environments.

The Greenhouse Complex consists of three large greenhouses and a small building for operations and storage; the Avian Cognition Laboratory (at left) is home to studies of seed caching and retrieval by pinyon jays and other birds (2008).

Ceramics Complex and Tea House

As an artistic discipline, ceramics appeared at NAU by the 1960s. The program operated a kiln behind the Fine Arts Building until the early 1980s. The ceramics studio relocated to several Stone Cottages and kiln operations moved under the east bleachers at Lumberjack Stadium, where they remained when the bleachers were removed; this became the Outback Studio. When the Stone Cottages disappeared in 1986, the ceramics studio joined the kilns on the east side of the stadium. For a time, a kiln for ceramics resided in the boiler area of the Plateau Center.

In the late 1980s, a dedicated set of structures and kilns were completed on the south periphery of campus, partially hidden by trees along Lone Tree Road. Kilns were brought to campus through collaboration between professor Don Bendel and Yukio Yamamoto, a Japanese devotee of the ancient art of Tozan pottery. Yamamoto received an honorary doctorate at the spring 1991 NAU commencement.

The complex involves eight kilns of varying types and sizes and a facility with teaching and faculty studios. Kilns are added over time, the most recent in 2005. The main building is styled in the transition from modern to postmodern architecture. Noteworthy are the cupola and tower, both of which are similarly oriented at an unusual angle to the tin roof. The windows represent the International style.

In 2002, a Japanese Tea House was fabricated adjoining the Ceramics Complex; there is also a garden. The Tea House is in honor of Yukio Yamamoto, the master potter who aided and inspired construction of the kilns.

The Ceramics Complex (2008), located on Lone Tree Road and behind the Capital Assets and Services Building on the southern end of campus, has several buildings with studios and a number of kilns. Shown here is one of the larger kilns.

A Japanese Tea House was constructed adjacent to the Ceramics Complex in 2002.

Recreation Center

Located adjacent to Lumberjack Stadium, the Recreation Center opened in 1989 with facilities for racquetball, basketball, and volleyball. It has a weight room, aerobic activities room, exercise equipment, offices, conference rooms, and locker rooms. The style is modern and very functional with a bold use of cement. A second gymnasium, added in 1994, cost $1.9 million. The facility is open to NAU students as part of the activity fee and to faculty and staff for an annual charge. Offices for Campus Recreation Services, the Fitness/ Wellness Program, NAU Outdoors, intramural sports, sports clubs, and the Child Enrichment Program are located here.

Many of these activities and offices were formerly located in the University Union Field House. As renovations to the Recreation Center commenced in summer 2009, recreation facilities and some of the associated programs returned, temporarily, to the Field House.

The Recreation Center and the Department of Athletics manage outdoor athletic fields. Among these are South Athletic Fields, Hilltop Fields, the field south of the Wall Aquatic Center, and a field next to the Atmospheric Research Observatory. The South Athletic Fields complex underwent extensive expansion in 2008–2009.

The Recreation Center (2008) prior to the 2009–2011 renovations.

Mountain View Hall

Views of the San Francisco Peaks and Mount Elden from this dormitory are spectacular. It is home for fraternities and sororities at NAU. In 1931, President Gammage approved the first fraternity. Soon, several fraternities occupied structures near campus, such as the Pi Kappa Epsilon House at 310 South Beaver Street, which is a private home today. Over the years, the number of fraternities increased slightly and several sororities debuted. By 1960, a decision to build on-campus housing for the Greek system resulted in two buildings, known as the Fraternity Dormitory and the Sorority Dormitory. The Fraternity Dorm became Raymond Hall in 1966. For a period beginning in the mid-1970s, the Sorority Dorm was the North Apartments; in 1989, it became McDonald Hall.

By 1964–1965, there were four fraternities and three sororities. This increased to twelve fraternities and four sororities by 1968–1969. The Greek system occupied a number of locations from the late 1960s through the 1970s. Sororities, all on campus, used Raymond Hall by the end of the decade, but earlier some were housed in McDonald, Stroud, and Morton Halls. Fraternities were located in Raymond, McDonald, Sechrist, and Stroud Halls, in Old Main, and at off-campus houses.

Plans for Mountain View Hall grew from a need for additional on-campus residences and for housing fraternities and sororities. The design incorporates an early postmodern style and transitional elements of postmodern architecture. Features include the glass entryway, multiple gables of varying sizes, and dormers. This structure opened for student use in 1990 and is more than simply functional—the building makes an architectural statement. It houses 574 students in suite-style arrangements with two bedrooms sharing a bathroom. There are conference rooms, chapter rooms, study areas, and a recreation facility.

Main entryway and portico of Mountain View Hall (2009), home of the Greek system at NAU.

Printing and Duplicating Services

Across Dupont Street from the Centennial and Wettaw Buildings are the offices for Printing and Duplicating Services. On site is a complete facility serving the campus for everything from envelopes and letterhead stationery to flyers, brochures, and magazines. There is a variety of state-of-the-art printing and bindery equipment. Customers from all areas of the campus receive expert assistance regarding design and execution of publications.

Prior to occupying this building, Printing and Duplicating was in several locations. For many years, these services were on the first floor of Gammage, near offices for the president and other administrators. They were also located in the basement of the NAU Bookstore, in portions of the North Union, and in several dormitories that comprise the Women's Quadrangle on the North Campus.

The current building for Printing and Duplicating was donated to NAU by George Babbitt's widow, Madeline, in 1991. Babbitt, a local postmaster and son of a Babbitt who came to Flagstaff in the 1880s, built the structure, which housed various businesses over several decades including a men's clothing store, jewelry store, barbershop, and restaurant. The opening of the jewelry store featured a 34-carat diamond, then valued at $70,000. Later a restaurant named the Chick-n-Bull operated here into the 1980s and regularly advertised in the student newspaper, the *Lumberjack*. Prior to its present use, Parking Services occupied portions of the complex.

The university's Printing Office (2008) is located in a former commercial building on Dupont Street.

Southwest Forest Science Complex

The Southwest Forest Science Complex, opened in 1992, is a partnership between the State of Arizona and the U.S. Forest Service. The forestry program began in 1959 and resided in the Blome Building. In 1960, Forestry moved to the Frier Building as the Science Building opened across North Campus. In 1962, the Forest Service constructed an office and laboratory facility next to Frier Hall (today's Geology Annex). With common interests and related missions, having these structures in close proximity was dynamic and productive.

When the need arose for additional space, fate stepped in and an even larger move occurred. The U.S. Forest Service headquarters for the southwestern United States was in Phoenix. As part of the construction of a new Southwest Forest Science Complex, these offices moved to Flagstaff.

The building is a state and federal partnership, with each government using half of the structure; they share the main lobby. The architecture is postmodern with continuing elements of simple and functional modernism. Postmodern features include its grand entryway and portico, a soldier belt course of bricks, bricks of different colors, and structural honesty with some I-beams visible. This structure has served as a home for several other campus units, including Geography and Public Planning, Parks and Recreation, and Applied Indigenous Studies.

A view of the NAU School of Forestry portion of the Southwest Forest Science Complex (2008).

Main entrance to the Southwest Forest Science Complex (2008). The U.S. Forest Service occupies the western portion of the building and the NAU School of Forestry is located in the eastern part of the structure.

THE UNIVERSITY CENTENNIAL AND TRANSITION TO A NEW MILLENNIUM

Two presidents, Clara Lovett and John Haeger, guided Northern Arizona University through the end of the twentieth century and the first decade of the twenty-first century. Near the end of the Lovett years, the Wettaw Building heralded a period of significant growth in the physical plant. During the first decade of the twenty-first century, new buildings included structures for business, science, and applied research and development. New residences, Pine Ridge Village and McKay Village, provide different, apartment-style housing for undergraduates. Aspen Crossing, a more traditional dormitory, opened in fall 2008. The university finished a parking garage in fall 2007, a harbinger of changes to come affecting traffic patterns around campus—a combination of bus service, bicycles, and walking will be the preferred modes of on-campus transportation, rather than personal cars. In addition, significant renovations for the Engineering and Communications Buildings, and a major addition to the University Union, were completed.

As construction and renovations progressed, the need for space to temporarily house students, staff, and faculty from various units necessitated "swing space"—locations to house those displaced by construction for periods ranging from months to several years. Initially, Bury Hall closed as a student residence and served as swing space. Soon, Peterson Hall shifted to use by displaced units. Since 2001, a complex of four buildings, collectively known as Emerald City, provides excellent swing space during construction.

Students returning for fall 2009 found ongoing and imminent projects including an expansion of South Athletic Fields, a Distance Learning addition to the Communications Building, and utilities expansions to accommodate new buildings. Additional projects scheduled soon are renovations to the Liberal Arts Building, safety improvements and new seating for Ardrey Auditorium, and safety improvements for the Walkup Skydome.

As NAU expands, new programs and changing technologies bring with them physical plant needs. An initiative in Applied Health Sciences will result in a structure to house existing programs such as Nursing, Dental Hygiene, and Physical Therapy as well as new programs in occupational therapy and training physician's assistants. The Recreation Center will expand to incorporate the Fronske Student Health Center, Counseling and Testing, classrooms, and Employee Assistance and Wellness. Centralization provides a more coordinated program of health and welfare services for students, staff, and faculty. Thanks to contributions from Arizona tribes, a Native American Center is slated for construction on land just west of the Liberal Arts Building.

The map (2008) and aerial photograph (2003) depict the location of the buildings that existed on campus up to 2008, covering the presidencies of Clara M. Lovett and John D. Haeger. All buildings highlighted in orange were constructed during the period 1993–2008. The map corresponds to chapter 5 of the text. Various buildings were added to the campus physical plant during these fifteen years to meet particular needs for academic buildings, service structures, student residence halls, a new conference center, and the first parking garage on campus. (A key for building numbers is on page 301.)

KNAU and Transportation Building

KNAU, the university-operated public radio station, shares this structure with the Mountain Campus Transit Bus Barn. It is a metal-sided, purely functional structure. KNAU, an affiliate of National Public Radio (NPR), was in the Communications Building until 1999, when it moved to South Campus.

Radio operations at NAU began with an on-campus student station in the 1950s. Over time, there were several such operations, using different call letters and operating at various frequencies, with internal campus networks and on a limited basis in the local area. Student-run operations included KASC, KAXR (the best remembered and one that broadcast locally), KRCK, and the current KJACK.

By the late 1970s, discussions favored a public radio broadcast facility for northern Arizona. A student radio station, with call letters KNAU, had operated since 1969. In 1980, the KAXR station ceased broadcasting and the KNAU call letters became the moniker for the public radio

station at the university. NAU submitted an application to join the NPR network. The process occurred in fits and starts, with funding needed for upgrades before the application could receive approval. KNAU, as a member of the NPR network, went on the air November 28, 1983, with a power of 100,000 watts. Initially, there was a transmitter on Mormon Mountain. By the first decade of the twenty-first century, there were transmitters in cities throughout northern Arizona. For a time, KNAU was the only NPR station between Albuquerque (east), Las Vegas (west), Phoenix (south), and Salt Lake City (north).

Plans for expanded KNAU operations envisioned a studio location on the second floor of the University Union Field House; this plan never materialized. Instead, when Speech Pathology moved from Performing and Fine Arts to Health Sciences on South Campus, the open space was reconfigured for KNAU. The station remained there from 1983 until it relocated to South Campus in 1999.

The National Public Radio (NPR) station for NAU shares this structure with Transportation Services (2008).

Sculpture Studio/
Recycling Building

This shedlike structure (2007) served as the university recycling center until 2006 and was then converted for use as the Sculpture Studio.

The Recycling Building, built in 1994, became the Sculpture Studio during summer 2006 with $330,000 in renovation costs. Its original function diminished when the university joined the City of Flagstaff to handle campus recycling needs. The architecture is a functional metal shed. Prior to making a new home in this structure, sculpture operations, often involving torches and flames (the sort of thing that makes administrators nervous), had homes behind the Performing and Fine Arts Building and in the Plateau Center.

Ponderosa Building

The Ponderosa Building sits on the western edge of campus, behind Ardrey Auditorium. It previously belonged to the Church of Jesus Christ of Latter-Day Saints (LDS), serving as a school and meeting center. Original construction, completed in 1968, is in the modern International style. NAU purchased the structure in 1997 and renamed it the Ponderosa Building. Half of the structure became home for Disability Resources, which provides testing and technology assistance, interpreters, and transportation assistance. The other half of the structure is a dance studio associated with Coconino Community College and the NAU Preparatory School.

The building's original purpose provides a window on the history of religion in association with the campus. Today, there is a Newman Center near the Ponderosa

Building and a Campus Ministries structure. Near the campus are buildings associated with LDS, the Baptist Student Center, and the Society of Friends. Andrew Peterson helped establish an Institute of Religion (also known as the LDS Institute). The LDS Building stood next to the College Inn, on the southeast corner of Dupont and Powers Streets. It opened in 1937 and remained in use for its original purpose until 1968.

Until the 1970s, the Institute of Religion offered classes in this structure and on campus. These received college credit and, with eighteen hours of coursework in religious studies, a student obtained a certificate. Each year, usually in the spring, there was a Religious Emphasis Week. Coverage of events for this week and other religious services and social events appeared regularly in the student newspaper.

The Ponderosa Building (late 1960s) as it neared completion as a school for the Church of Jesus Christ of Latter-Day Saints.

The Ponderosa Building (2008), from the same perspective as the preceding photo.
This building is now home for NAU Disability Resources and a dance studio.

Wastewater Treatment Demonstration Facility

Civil and Environmental Engineering established a Wastewater Demonstration Program in a woody area on South Campus, between the Capital Assets and Services Building and the South Apartments. The university, the Arizona Department of Environmental Quality (ADEQ), and the U.S. Environmental Protection Agency fund the site. It serves as a demonstration and training facility, geared to enhancing treatment of residential wastewater and improving the quality of groundwater. A limited research program is also part of this facility.

Centennial Building

Completed in time for the NAU Centennial (1999), this structure houses Human Resources and Parking Services. Human Resources involves payroll and employee relations—hiring of faculty and staff, training and professional development, and benefits services. Prior to this location, Parking Services had space under the west side of Lumberjack Stadium, in what is now Printing and Duplicating Services, and in apartments located on Ellery Street. The building design is quintessential postmodern with a white cornice line and large pediments above the windows. It is a simplified revival of the earlier twentieth-century fascination with Colonial Revival. The curved stone banner bearing the university's name and the building itself provide a distinctive north entrance to the campus.

The Centennial Building, completed in the year of NAU's hundredth anniversary (1999), houses Human Resources and Parking Services.

Wettaw Biology and Biochemistry Building

At the close of the twentieth century, the Biology (1967), Chemistry (1968), and Science (1960) Buildings exceeded capacity, were facing safety issues, and needed modern equipment. In 1997, under the guidance of President Clara Lovett, planning began for a facility that was later named the Wettaw Biology and Biochemistry Building. Students and faculty in Biological Sciences and Chemistry and Biochemistry share the building, which opened in 2000. Architecturally, the Wettaw Building is postmodern with polychrome facades. The entrance is neoclassical themed with columns that mirror those on Campbell Hall. The stonework of the circular exterior of the lecture hall is an Italian diaper pattern. A sky bridge links the Wettaw structure to Chemistry, both physically and historically, in that one can view buildings representing two dominant architectural eras in America—the modernist era of the Chemistry Building and the Wettaw Building as representative of the more ornamental, postmodern era.

Housed in this building are four teaching laboratories, a 254-seat lecture hall, research support facilities, ten research laboratories, offices, and a conference room. Two to four scientists, their graduate and undergraduate students, and staff share a laboratory space. Collaborations involving faculty within and between departments provide excellent training opportunities for students and result in considerable external funding of research. During the last decade, NAU increased its involvement in biotechnology, producing several patented inventions and training the future workforce with state-of-the-art technology.

As with any construction project, there are glitches. The Wettaw Building was no exception. As the project was nearing completion, an inspection revealed that of the three major power panels, two were refurbished versions of older models; the electrical subcontractor went bankrupt and did not provide specified power panels. Earlier in construction, after pouring an entire second floor of cement, there was concern, during the cold-weather snap at the time, that the wrong mixture was used and the floor might have to be jackhammered out and redone. Samples sent for testing confirmed that everything was in order and construction proceeded.

Biography

John F. Wettaw was born on April 17, 1939, in St. Louis, Missouri; grew up in Eldorado, Illinois, and attended public schools there; and received his bachelor of science in chemistry at Southern Illinois University in 1961. After obtaining a doctorate at Michigan State University in 1967, he completed a National Science Foundation postdoctoral fellowship at Texas A&M University. Wettaw joined the faculty at Northern Arizona University in 1967, where he remained for forty years. Even in retirement, Wettaw continues to teach several courses each semester and during summer school. He is renowned for classroom teaching and for his ability to

John F. Wettaw, longtime, highly respected teacher at NAU and prominent member of the Arizona State Legislature.

remember students. He served as chair of the Department of Chemistry and Biochemistry from 2002 to 2005.

In addition to his academic duties, Wettaw entered politics, winning election to the Arizona House of Representatives from Coconino County in 1972. He was District 2 representative in the state legislature from 1973 to 1992 and then entered the Arizona State Senate, serving from 1993 to 2001. During his long tenure in Phoenix, he held numerous key committee assignments, including chair of the Joint Committee on Capital Review, chair of the Joint Legislative Budget Committee, and chair of the

Appropriations Committee of the House. He also was president pro tem of the state senate. Wettaw remains an ardent supporter of education and of NAU. As part of his farewell from the legislature, his colleagues approved an appropriation of $750,000 to provide new equipment for the Biology and Biochemistry Building named in his honor. He has served on the boards of several local organizations, including the Rotary Club and the Grand Canyon Boy Scout Council. John Wettaw received an honorary degree from NAU at the May 2008 commencement, where he was also the speaker.

269

The Wettaw Biology and Biochemistry Building (2007), looking to the northeast, with the lecture hall on the right and a wing with student laboratories and research facilities on the left. The Printing and Duplicating Services Building is visible in the left rear of the photograph. (Photo courtesy of Helen Long.)

Emerald City

Emerald City (2008), consisting of four similar structures and located on South Campus near Transportation Services, serves as swing space, housing various departments and units for periods of time during new construction or renovation.

As renovations and new construction reached a fever pitch early in the new millennium, Peterson and Bury Halls became swing space for use by units displaced by this activity. When more swing space was needed, a separate set of buildings, dubbed Emerald City, opened for use in 2003 on South Campus.

Four similar, purely functional structures, labeled A–D, all frame buildings, have green and tan, earth-tone color schemes, blending with the surroundings. The buildings house faculty offices, departmental offices, computing labs, classrooms, and two seminar rooms.

Several departments rotated through Emerald City in its first years, including the School of Communications and part of the College of Engineering, both displaced while complete remodels with additions occurred in their home buildings. With demolition of the Anthropology Building to make room for the new W. A. Franke College of Business Administration, the anthropologists moved to Emerald City, where they remain today. Also housed here, on a more permanent basis, are the Program in Intensive English (PIE) and the Center for Data Insight.

Pine Ridge Village Apartments

No dormitory construction took place on the NAU campus between the time Mountain View Hall opened (1990) and the early years of the twenty-first century. During that time, features that are attractive to students changed. The shift in student desires led to new designs for living spaces. The need for different types of residences for students brought about some innovative public/private partnerships. Pine Ridge Village/Campus Heights LLC and Northern Arizona University operate Pine Ridge Village Apartments, located in the shadows of the Walkup Skydome on South Campus.

Pine Ridge Village, opened for fall 2004, features postmodern architecture incorporating a touch of the earlier Craftsman Bungalow and Colonial styles. There are other hints at historic elements, including keystones above the windows, rooflines with multiple gables, and large plate-glass windows. The complex contains twelve buildings with a mix of twelve or eighteen apartments per structure, for a total capacity of 336 students. Each apartment has four single bedrooms, two full bathrooms, a well-equipped kitchen, a living/dining area, and a washer/dryer combination. The community center for the complex has a workout room, recreation area, study room, and television area.

Pine Ridge Village Apartments (2008) is a new concept for the new millennium, with apartment-style living in a beautiful grove of ponderosa pines between the Walkup Skydome and McConnell Hall.

Hogan

The Hogan has an octagonal configuration and an east-facing entrance, hidden by the tree in this view.

In 2003, a traditional Navajo hogan was constructed on a knoll south of the Southwest Forest Science Complex. The structure serves for small gatherings, particularly in connection with the Applied Indigenous Studies Program. It also accommodates traditional Navajo observances. Northern Arizona University has several resident elders at any one time from different Arizona Indian tribes, who serve as a bridge between two worlds for students and aid in spiritual and practical matters, providing comfort and cultural knowledge to all students in need.

W. A. Franke College of Business Administration Building

In 2006, NAU opened a new College of Business Administration Building, the third structure to bear this name. The first two are the Adel Mathematics Building (used 1953–1972) and Social and Behavioral Sciences West (used 1972–2005). Until 1930, classes in business topics were taught in Old Main, then the Library and Administration Building (Gammage) from 1930 to 1945, and back to Old Main until 1953. Initially, the unit name involved the word "commerce" until 1930, when it became the Department of Business Education (1931–1941), then reverted to Commerce for the period 1941–1959, before being called the Division of Business for four years (1959–1963) and the School of Business Administration (1963–1966). In 1966, it became the College of Business Administration. A gift of $25 million in late spring 2007 from Phoenix businessman William A. Franke provided for student scholarships, faculty development, and curriculum development in business. The gift resulted in a name change to the W. A. Franke College of Business Administration.

Designed to look north to the San Francisco Peaks, the structure fits into a postmodern style of glass, brick, and metal, with a sleek, smooth, and shiny facade. The structure has an environmentally conspicuous design, much like the New Laboratory Facility on North Campus. It received the Arizona Public Service 2006 Energy Award. Features of the building foster personal interactions, including wide stairwells, seating arrangements in open spaces, places where students can plug in laptop computers, and areas outside each classroom where students and professors can continue discussions after lectures. Jazzman's Café, located near a first-floor lounge area, further enhances this atmosphere of open communication and dialogue. This building signifies NAU's incorporation of the latest trend for interior college building design, that of using interior spaces to promote student and faculty conversations and to encourage a learning-oriented environment that contrasts sharply with the stark, modernist hallways of the past.

Other building occupants include the NAU Elderhostel Program, the Arizona Rural Policy Institute, the Center for American Indian Economic Development, and the Bureau of Economic Research. In addition to office and classroom spaces, the Gardner Auditorium is a memorial to Larry and Barbara Gardner, who died tragically in 1989.

Biographies

William A. Franke was born in Texas and grew up in Brazil, where he graduated from high school. He received undergraduate and graduate degrees from Stanford University. He began his career as a lawyer with a practice centering on real estate and finance. He served in the U.S. Navy during the Vietnam War.

During a distinguished career, Franke held positions with major firms and founded or co-founded a number of businesses and investment firms. Among these firms are Southwest Forest Industries (CEO), Valley National Bank (chair, Executive Committee), Circle K Company (chair), and America West Airlines (CEO—now U.S. Airways). He was founding chair for Airplanes Group, a major aircraft finance and investment fund. He was involved with Ryanair, Gate Gourmet (airline food services), Beringer Winery, and ON Semiconductor. Currently, William Franke serves as chair for, or on the board of, companies around the world:

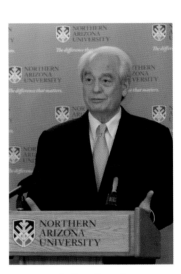

William A. Franke, whose 2007 gift to Northern Arizona University provided the opportunity to rename the College of Business Administration in his honor.

A view of the W. A. Franke College of Business Administration (2007), looking north across the grassy quadrangle on South Campus.

Tiger Airways (Singapore), Bristol Group (Argentina), Spirit Airlines (United States), Mandala Airlines (Indonesia), Wizz Air (Hungary), and the investment firm Indigo Partners.

Franke is a strong civic presence—he serves as chair of the Greater Phoenix Leadership group (formerly called the Phoenix 40) and on boards and councils for Arizona State University, Barrow Neurological Institute, and Stanford Law School, as well as being a patron of the arts. Prior to the $25 million gift to Northern Arizona University, Franke established scholarships for minority students at the University of Arizona and Arizona State University. The gift to NAU will support visits to the university by eminent scholars, maintaining technology in the college, ethics education, and promotion of curricular emphasis on communications skills.

Larry and Barbara Gardner, for whom the W. A. Franke College of Business Administration auditorium is named, were found dead on September 26, 1989, killed tragically by their son. Larry Gardner was born on November 7, 1936, in Sidney, Iowa, where he completed high school in 1955. He received his bachelor of science in education from Northwest Missouri State College (University) and his master of arts from the University of Missouri at Columbia. Larry did additional study at Arizona State University and was a certified public accountant. He taught classes in financial and managerial accounting and in auditing and was the adviser to Alpha Sigma Pi, the accounting fraternity. He was a gifted teacher. He occasionally jumped on a desk or table to make a point. He also got down on his knees to plead with students attempting to leave class early to "please stay." Larry Gardner received the President's Award for Faculty and Academic Professionals for 1986–1987.

Barbara Gardner was born on August 18, 1941, in St. Louis, Missouri, where she completed high school in 1960. She received a bachelor's degree from Southeast Missouri State College in 1964. Barbara was a nurse at Flagstaff Medical Center and a leader for Planned Parenthood. The Gardners were well known for civic involvement and for their generosity, always happy to open their home to students.

Gardner Auditorium in the W. A. Franke College of Business Administration is named to honor Larry Gardner, who taught in the College of Business for many years, and his wife, Barbara.

A view of the north facade of the W. A. Franke College of Business Administration (2007), showing the extensive use of glass on this side of the building.

McKay Village Apartments

As noted in the entry for Pine Ridge Village Apartments, student housing preferences shifted over the past twenty years. Many now choose to live in apartment-style accommodations. Until recently, most such housing was available only off campus, in the surrounding community. With the opening of Pine Ridge Village in fall 2004 and soon thereafter the McKay Village Apartments, the university now offers additional housing options.

Todd Associates designed this $30 million complex in much the same style as Pine Ridge Village—the epitome of postmodern design, which looks to the past for inspiration. In this case, the popular Craftsman Bungalow style dominates the design, mirroring a national revival trend of the Craftsman movement from a century earlier. McKay Village can be interpreted as a new-urbanist community within a larger university campus, oriented toward historic architecture, central green space, and a community center, with access to the entire campus by walking or biking.

There are twelve buildings containing 132 two-, three-, and four-bedroom apartments, providing accommodations for 444 students. Juniors, seniors, and graduate students live in these units, which are equipped much like those in Pine Ridge Village.

Biography

Kay E. McKay began an extended career with Big Brothers Big Sisters of Flagstaff in the 1960s, and she has served this organization for more than forty years. She co-founded Big Sisters in 1964 and was the first executive director. In 1967, she and her husband, David, founded Big Brothers Big Sisters of Flagstaff. They celebrated the fortieth anniversary of this combined organization in 2007. McKay remains the executive director of Big Brothers Big Sisters of Flagstaff. This nonprofit service organization is part of a national organization that is the largest and oldest program in the United States for mentoring children to provide a basis for lasting impacts on their development and strong, positive relationships to others and their community.

Kay McKay has a remarkable record of local and statewide service. In the Flagstaff and northern Arizona community, she worked with Flagstaff Medical Center and Northern Arizona Healthcare as a mediator for Coconino County Superior Court, and as chair of the NAU Social and Behavioral Sciences Leadership Team. She was a member of ABOR for eight years, including one as president. She was national vice chair of the executive directors of Big Brothers Big Sisters and is a member of the ADA–Coda Commission. McKay has a strong reputation as a motivational speaker and professional development consultant. She provides seminars and workshops on topics pertaining to a healthy workplace environment and increased productivity.

Her honors and accolades include the 1984 Big Brothers Big Sisters of America Margaret Slack Award, 1994 Flagstaff Citizen of the Year, 1995 Soroptimist International Woman of the Year Award, and the Athena Business Woman of the Year Award in 1990 from the Flagstaff Chamber of Commerce. McKay received an honorary degree from NAU in 2004.

Kay McKay, former member of the Arizona Board of Regents and prominent Flagstaff citizen.

A view of the multicolored units that comprise the McKay Village Apartments (2008).

Parking Structure

Concern for conservation of natural resources and environmental preservation, combined with the parking problem present on most college campuses, spurred the decisions for a parking structure. It exemplifies postmodern architecture with interesting visual detail and opened in fall 2007 with more than seven hundred parking spaces on three levels.

The master plan for the NAU campus includes a reduction in vehicular traffic throughout Central Campus. A second parking structure is part of the High Country Conference Center and associated Drury Inn & Suites at the northern edge of campus, on land that was formerly a large surface parking lot.

The first campus parking structure opened in fall 2007. The pedestrian bridge to Ardrey Auditorium is visible on the right side of the photograph.

New Laboratory Facility

A variety of forces converged and led to construction of the New Laboratory Facility, which opened in stages, beginning in 2007, and is shared by the Departments of Biological Sciences and Chemistry and Biochemistry. Among these were life safety issues, particularly in the existing Chemistry Building; a need for state-of-the-art technology for classroom laboratories and research; and an increase in student enrollments in science. A key feature is liberal use of open spaces with comfortable seating and movable whiteboards for writing. The first-floor atrium houses a coffee shop.

The structure features a postmodern design with elements reminiscent of the International style. There are no innovations incorporating historic styles, many features involve rounded components, and there is a variety of facade types. The building is futuristic in appearance, but very functional in overall design. In addition to the building costs, $5.2 million of funds paid for research equipment, compliance with safety and regulatory concerns, laboratory furnishings, and audio-visual equipment. To prepare for the New Laboratory Facility, Hanley Hall was razed. A significant portion of the Moenkopi sandstone from the outer walls of Hanley Hall was preserved and is used in the walls on the east side of the building. A plaque denoting the former location of Hanley Hall and paying homage to Margaret ("Mother") Hanley is in the atrium of the new structure and an outdoor memorial is located on the lawn west of the new building.

East face of the New Laboratory Facility on North Campus (2008).

Applied Research and Development Building

At the close of the twentieth century, new developments in biotechnology and commercialization ventures occasioned the need for a facility devoted to research applications combined with basic science. NAU's growing commitment to sustainable living and a neutral carbon footprint provided an opportunity to construct a model building incorporating features for the protection of natural resources. The Applied Research and Development (ARD) Building, opened in spring 2007, is a LEED (Leadership in Energy and Environmental Design) platinum-certified building, one of just a few such structures at academic institutions in the United States. To obtain such a lofty rating, a building must accumulate points for aspects of its construction and design.

The ARD Building features a functional, modernist design that is, most importantly, environmentally sustainable. The sweeping, three-story, curved atrium facing south bears the name Arizona Public Service (APS) Atrium to honor the contributions made to building construction and its energy-saving features.

To obtain these accolades, the building includes water recycling, energy-saving features such as passive solar heating, reuse of building materials, recycling of construction waste materials, extensive use of natural daylight, and wood purchased from a sustainable forest managed by the White Mountain Apache Tribe. A portion of the electricity comes from solar energy generated by a panel array on South Campus, next to Interstate 40. The concrete contains 40 percent fly ash (the waste generated from coal-fired electric plants) obtained from the coal-fired power plant at Joseph City, and the exterior paving is porous to reduce runoff. Built on the site of a retention basin, the landscaping incorporates indigenous vegetation that needs little irrigation. Building temperature is maintained by innovative technologies, including a heat exchanger, automated windows, shade controls, and a backup heating system of solar thermal panels on the roof. In total, 75 percent of the illumination comes from daylight, and there is an overall 40 percent energy savings for the building.

Among its occupants are the Pathogen Genomics Institute, Center for Environmental Genetics and Genomics, Office of the Vice President for Research, Office of Grant and Contract Services, Office of Sponsored Projects, Center for Sustainable Environments, Center for Ecological Monitoring and Assessment, Geospatial Research and Information Laboratory, and Merriam-Powell Center for Environmental Research. In keeping with the conservation mission, a new Office of Sustainability was established in this building.

The Applied Research and Development Building opened in late spring 2007. It is the first campus Leadership in Energy and Environmental Design (LEED) platinum-certified building.

High Country Conference Center

Over a period of ten years, the NAU administration and City of Flagstaff considered ideas for a conference center. In the end, a combined conference center and hotel resulted from a partnership among the university, the city, and a private developer. A parking garage adjoins the convention facilities and hotel. The State of Arizona purchased much of the site in 1953 for $30,000. Facilities in the conference center include a Grand Ballroom that can seat up to one thousand people for lectures or eight hundred for banquets. The ballroom can convert into up to five smaller rooms for sessions of one hundred to two hundred people. A boardroom can accommodate one hundred people, and five additional rooms, each seating fifty to seventy-five people, are located in the Drury Inn & Suites across an elevated walkway.

Criticized and praised for its design and for its prominent location on West Butler Avenue (easily accessible from Interstates 17 and 40), the High Country Conference Center makes a bold statement. The conference/hotel complex certifies that the era of "simple, modern glass boxes" is gone for good. Unlike its modernist predecessors, this place is designed to be noticed, with its thoroughly postmodern exaggeration of an Italianate-style cornice line

on the hotel, brightly colored brick facade, and a rather massive scale compared to other local structures. The design is not unique, however, but a version of similar contemporary highway hotel and conference center architecture seen in projects across the nation.

Like its dominating architecture, the location stirred discussion and controversy. Some claim the view of historical North Campus is blocked from Butler Avenue, as is the view of the San Francisco Peaks from the North Campus, while new-urbanist proponents claim the "infill" location to be perfect, within walking distance to downtown and NAU attractions.

The High Country Conference Center opened in late March 2008. The Drury Inn & Suites portion of the complex has 160 rooms, designed by Drury architects with assistance from Shepherd-Wesnitzer Inc. of Flagstaff. Drury Southwest contractors fabricated the hotel at a cost of $8.5 million.

In addition to providing convention accommodations, the hotel and conference center serve as training facilities for NAU students in the Eugene M. Hughes School of Hotel and Restaurant Management as well as a location for gatherings of local organizations.

Opposite: The High Country Conference Center (2008) and the adjacent Drury Inn & Suites provide a state-of-the-art facility for conferences and meetings. (Photo by Tom Alexander.)

Aspen Crossing Learning Community

As the demand for on-campus housing grew, NAU added Pine Ridge Village Apartments and the McKay Village Apartments. During the researching and writing of this book, heavy machinery on a plot of land near Raymond Hall and the Gateway Student Center near the middle of campus signaled another construction project. Open for fall 2008, the new residence hall, with suites, accommodates 348 students and is academically focused. It has a quiet environment and considers applications for residence from students with minimum GPAs of 3.0.

A decided improvement over the expansive parking lot that once occupied this space, the new Aspen Crossing Learning Community blends well with surrounding, earlier modernist buildings. This largely functional structure is nearly square and includes three floors of living and community gathering spaces for residents. Aside from its contemporary construction materials, the building essentially represents a twenty-first-century version of International-style architecture. The primary facade on all four sides consists of a deep-red brick facing, the walls broken periodically with even-spaced picture windows for the student living spaces. Two porches were built into the south corners of the building, and the structure's most prominent feature involves an impressive three-story, vaulted atrium for the northwest corner, promising its residents breathtaking views of the San Francisco Peaks and the western sky. Large plate-glass windows held together with standard metal mullions enclose the atrium.

The Aspen Crossing residence hall was completed in summer 2008 and students moved in during August of the same year.

CAMPUS ROADWAYS

Over the course of the first century and more of NAU, a number of roadways on campus were named to honor those who served the university in various ways. The map shows existing campus roadways in blue, former campus roadways that no longer exist in pink, and roadways that connect the campus with the city of Flagstaff in orange.

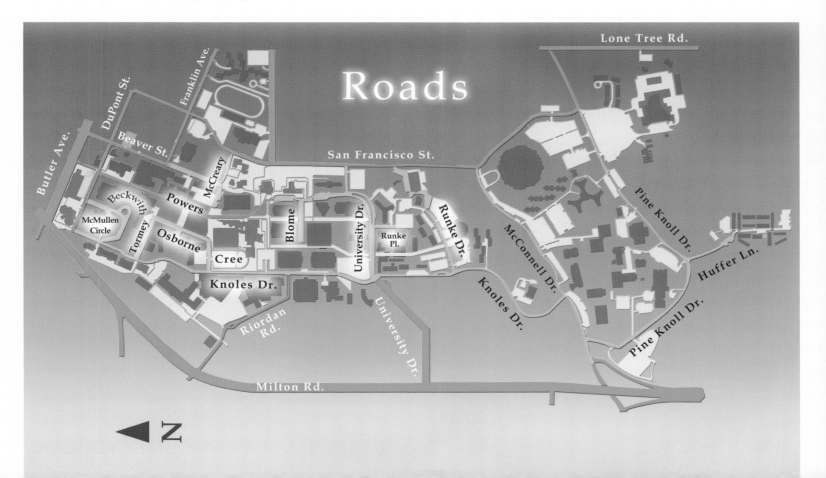

288

For each roadway, its location is given and a brief biography tells of those for whom the streets are named.

Beckwith Drive

A small circle at the northeast corner of the North Campus; around the circle are Bury Hall, the New Laboratory Facility, and Campbell Hall.

Biography

Catherine Mary Beckwith was born in Erie, Pennsylvania, in 1874. After thirty-eight years in the eastern United States, she moved to Arizona in 1912, just as it became a state. After living in Winslow for several years, Beckwith moved to Flagstaff. She was housemother for various dormitories from 1916 to 1941, including Campbell Hall, the Women's Quadrangle, and, briefly, Taylor Hall, a men's dormitory. Catherine Beckwith was homecoming dedicatee for 1941, her twenty-fifth year with the college.

She appeared on an episode of the television show *This Is Your Life* in 1955 honoring Andy Devine, who was an ASTCF student when Beckwith was a housemother. She lived long enough to have great-grandchildren and died at the Arizona Pioneers' Home in Prescott in late November 1965.

Blome Drive

This short road is just south of Raymond and McDonald Halls.

Biography

See Blome Building (Teacher Training School) in chapter 1.

Catherine Beckwith was a house resident on the campus from 1916 until 1941, serving in all three houses of the Women's Quadrangle on North Campus and then, briefly, in Taylor Hall.

Cree Drive

This short drive, which no longer exists, followed the contour of the Stone Cottages (which were located on today's Central Campus) from 1939 or 1940 until the 1980s.

Biography

Robert Boone Cree was superintendent of buildings and grounds from 1922 until 1949. Born on September 9, 1876, in Georgetown, Colorado, he came to Arizona in 1894, passing through Flagstaff and settling in the Phoenix area. He was a delivery boy for a period and then was in the mining and assessment business with his brother near Prescott. He served as elected justice of the peace in Bagdad, Arizona, a copper-mining community, and later ran a grocery store in Ray, Arizona. He also operated a hauling service between Jerome and Phoenix via the old Black Canyon Highway. His twenty-seven years as buildings superintendent at Flagstaff produced a strong reputation for "getting the job done and done right." After retirement and the loss of his wife, Robert Cree moved to Madison, New Jersey, to live with his son's family. He died there on May 27, 1956.

Robert Cree (at left) served as superintendent of buildings and grounds for the college from the 1920s through the 1940s.

Huffer Lane

This pathway connects Pine Knoll Drive to the South Apartments.

Biography

Harold L. Huffer was a member of the Arizona House of Representatives from Coconino County, beginning in 1965. He was a strong advocate of the college and of the plan to establish the South Academic Center.

Knoles Drive

Knoles Drive is a major north–south artery on the western side of campus, connecting Dupont Avenue to McConnell Drive.

Biography

Thomas M. Knoles Jr. moved with his family from Los Angeles to the Huachuca Mountains, where they operated a small cattle ranch between 1916 and the early 1920s. He attended high school in Tucson and graduated from Flagstaff High School in 1924. The senior Knoles started a bakery in 1923, which operated until 1945. Thomas Jr. worked at the bakery and assisted with opening and operating a second bakery in Warren, Arizona. He then returned to Flagstaff and purchased the Peerless Bakery. As a large, primarily wholesale operation, it provided baked goods to local businesses and to trading posts throughout the Navajo Nation and Hopi Reservation. Breads were shipped out via parcel post and payments often consisted of Navajo rugs and Native American goods in lieu of cash.

Knoles helped start the Native American Pow Wow in 1932 and served for several decades on the board of directors for the sponsoring organization. He entered politics in 1955 and served six years in the Arizona House of Representatives and then five terms in the Arizona State Senate, where he chaired the Appropriations Committee. He married Eleanor Greenlaw, from a pioneer Flagstaff family, and built a large, rustic home on Greenlaw family land. Thomas Knoles Jr. died in Phoenix in November 1984.

McConnell Drive

This roadway runs eastward from the southwest campus entrance to South San Francisco Street by the Walkup Skydome.

Biography

See McConnell Hall in chapter 3.

Harold Huffer served in the Arizona State Legislature, where he was an energetic supporter of the college and of establishing the South Academic Center.

Thomas Knoles Jr. was a member of a family that operated bakeries in Flagstaff and northern Arizona. He served as a primary organizer of the annual Native American Pow Wow held in Flagstaff for more than thirty years. Knoles served sixteen years in the state house and senate in Phoenix.

McCreary Street

McCreary Street at one time traversed the campus between Beaver Street and Knoles Drive. Two sections remain, between Knoles and Osborne Drives and from Beaver Street to the parking lot between Babbitt Academic Annex and Peterson Hall.

Biography

Aaron McCreary obtained his master of science in physical education at the University of Southern California. He coached baseball at Tucson High School, leading the team to an 8–3 championship in 1922, and moved to the State Teachers College at Tempe as a coach and director of athletics. He coached football, basketball, and baseball. In 1931, he came to Flagstaff as an associate coach and director of physical education. His career at the college included stints coaching football, basketball (1931–1940), and track and field and as director of athletics. McCreary spent forty-three years in athletic coaching and administration, thirty-two of those at Flagstaff, before retiring in 1963.

McCreary entered the U.S. Army during World War II as a first lieutenant stationed at Fort Sill, Oklahoma, and then as part of the Army Air Corps. He attained the rank of captain and then major in December 1944. He returned to coaching and teaching at Arizona State College at Flagstaff in 1946. A highlight of his career was initiating the college ski team, accomplished on June 9, 1938, at Schultz Pass. Yes, the date is correct! In January 1939, he took the ski team to Hart Prairie for additional training. McCreary was the homecoming dedicatee in 1955. Aaron "Mac" McCreary was inducted posthumously into the NAU Hall of Fame in 1981.

Aaron "Mac" McCreary was a coach at the school for many years, piloting teams in a variety of sports, and also served as athletic director. His career at the university spanned thirty-two years.

McMullen Circle

McMullen Circle is a short road through the historic North Campus, intersecting Beckwith Drive and traversing past North Union and North Morton Hall.

Biography

See McMullen Wall in chapter 1.

Osborne Drive

This roadway connects McCreary Street and Tormey Avenue (the terms "avenue," "drive," and "street" are sometimes used interchangeably when referring to the roadways named for McCreary and Tormey). The Adel Mathematics Building is to the west and the Plateau Center is to the east.

Biography

Francis C. (Doc) Osborn (Osborn spelled his name without the "e") was born on March 27, 1893, in Syracuse, New York. He received his bachelor of arts degree from Columbia University and a master of science in education from Northern Colorado State Teachers College (Northern Colorado University). Osborn served in the U.S. Navy during World War I and established a manual arts rehabilitation program for veterans at Fort Whipple in Prescott, Arizona. He joined the NANS faculty in 1923 and, in the years following the war, ASCF became a leader in the field of manual arts therapy.

Osborn was head of the industrial arts program, making it among the best in the Southwest. He was the first industrial arts education teacher from Arizona elected to membership in Epsilon Pi Tau, the international honor society for technology professions. Osborn's role at ASCF extended to athletics, where he represented the school at the founding of the Border Athletic Conference in 1931; he served as the conference's president in 1938 and 1946. When ASCF joined the Frontier Conference in 1952, he became president and served until 1959.

Osborn was a member of the Veterans of Foreign Wars and the American Legion (including a stint as local commander) and served as president of the local Kiwanis Club. He died on February 6, 1973, in Flagstaff.

Francis Osborn was a distinguished and long-serving member of the Arizona State College at Flagstaff faculty in the area of manual arts, also called industrial arts. He was also active in the field of athletics and helped form the Border Athletic Conference.

Powers Road

This road no longer exists. Formerly, it ran south through campus from Dupont Avenue to McCreary Street, effectively as an extension of Humphreys Street; the pedway through North Campus follows the course of the old Powers Road.

Biography

Robert R. Powers was born and raised in Eddyville, Iowa, receiving his high school diploma there in 1911. He graduated with a bachelor of science degree from Drake University in Des Moines in 1916, majoring in physics and minoring in mathematics. After graduation and before U.S. Army service in World War I, Powers was an instructor at Drake and taught high school in Sumner, Iowa. Immediately following the war, he held positions as superintendent of schools for Auburn and then Lisbon, Iowa. He joined NANS in 1922 and taught mathematics. In 1927, he added the duties of college registrar, a position he held for nearly two decades.

Powers was an ardent supporter of outdoor activities. He headed the local hiking club and led camping tours of the region. His real love was skiing; in 1939–1940, he helped with the original work for what is now the Snow Bowl—he mapped out the first four trails. Powers was a member of the National Ski Patrol and a founder and officer of the Flagstaff Ski Club. At the outset of World War II, Powers aided in training soldiers equipped with skis, a deployment that became the 10th Mountain Division.

Locally, he was a founder of the Kiwanis Club and a member of the Elks and helped originate the annual Forty-Niner Days that became the annual Native American Pow Wow. Robert Powers died on June 26, 1944, in Culver City, California, in his early fifties.

Robert Powers served the college for more than two decades, initially as a teacher of mathematics and then, for much of his career, as registrar. He was very involved in local civic and outdoor activities.

Runke Drive and Runke Place

Runke Drive is a serpentine and fragmented path, with one section beginning at Knoles Drive near Campus Heights Apartments and then traversing eastward past the Bilby Center, McKay Village Apartments, the Anthropology Laboratory, and the ROTC/Property Control Building. A second section travels south from University Drive into the McKay Village Apartments. Runke Place, south of the apartment complex, no longer exists.

Biography

Walter Runke Jr. was born on August 3, 1909, in Panguitch, Utah. In 1914, the family moved to Tuba City, Arizona, where his father was the Indian agent for Western Navajo Agency until 1920. The family moved to Flagstaff that year and his father became postmaster. Runke received his bachelor of arts in civil engineering and worked as a mechanic at the local Studebaker garage from 1933 to 1942. After a brief period as the maintenance mechanic at Babbitt Brothers Trading Company, Runke began employment with ASTCF in late 1942. He held the position of buildings and grounds superintendent and supervised preparation of sites for the federal housing and instruction buildings moved to the campus just after World War II. He was buildings and grounds superintendent until his death on January 29, 1963, at his home in Flagstaff.

Walter Runke was a dynamic member of the Townjacks, which supported college athletics, and a leader of the Flagstaff Lodge of Free and Accepted Masons (F&AM). He died during his second term on the Flagstaff school board.

Walter Runke Jr. joined Arizona State Teachers College at Flagstaff in 1942 and served the school for more than two decades as superintendent of buildings and grounds.

Tormey Avenue

This roadway travels between Knoles and Osborne Drives, behind the Ashurst Building, Old Main, and Taylor Hall.

Biography

Thomas J. Tormey served as ASTCF president from 1933 until 1944. He was born on August 13, 1891, in Missouri Valley, Iowa. His father was with the railroad and the family moved frequently during his youth, mostly in Illinois and Wisconsin. When his parents divorced, Tormey and his mother lived in small towns in Iowa and Nebraska. He received his high school diploma in Missouri Valley in 1908. He worked his way through Coe College in Cedar Rapids, Iowa, graduating with a bachelor of science in 1914. His work experiences included stoking furnaces, selling shoes, and using his chemistry major testing ore samples.

Tormey taught school and became superintendent in Independence, Iowa. He joined the U.S. Army in 1917 and served in the Army Air Corps. He was in flight training when the armistice occurred. After the war, he was school superintendent in Grundy Center, Iowa, for ten years. Tormey enrolled in the graduate program at the University of Iowa and completed his doctorate in 1932. A year later, he became the eighth president of the college at Flagstaff.

Tormey's years at the helm witnessed changes in physical plant and curriculum. The Women's Quadrangle on North Campus was finished with North Hall and the connector between Morton and Campbell Halls. Tormey was the first president to use the sale of bonds to raise funds for capital construction. A $250,000 bond issue provided much of the funding for constructing North Hall. The power plant was enlarged, Cottage City began, and the Training School was remodeled. During his tenure, the master of science in education debuted, the first forestry classes began, and the Navy V-12 unit came to campus in the early 1940s.

Tormey served as vice chair of the Civilian Defense Program for northern Arizona. In 1943, he took a leave to do defense work in Pasadena, California; he resigned in June 1944 and Tom O. Bellwood, the interim president, received the permanent appointment. Tormey spent the remainder of his career working in industry at various locations in California. He died in Altadena, California, in 1988 at ninety-seven years of age.

Thomas Tormey was the eighth president of Arizona State Teachers College at Flagstaff, serving from 1933 to 1944, including much of the Great Depression and World War II.

∼

Northern Arizona University has gone through many changes in name, in mission, and in terms of the physical plant. This book provides a comprehensive look at the manner in which the buildings developed on the campus, beginning with Old Main and traveling up to the present with the opening of the Aspen Crossing residence hall in fall 2008. Following this path of more than a century of development, several trends emerge.

Campus Expansion

The most noticeable change is the expansion of the campus, primarily southward. Almost all the buildings of the institution up until the 1930s were in an area known as the Old Campus or North Campus. In the late 1930s, the Stone Cottages were constructed, not far south of McMullen Field and the Riles Building. After World War II, some temporary structures provided housing for veterans, as enrollment swelled at Arizona State College. These initiated the southward expansion of the campus.

In the period from 1948 to 1953, the campus expansion included completion of Frier Hall as the home for the science curriculum, Lumberjack Gymnasium, the North Union with Prochnow Auditorium, and a new heating plant, located just south of the gym. The next major addition to the campus was the Eastburn Education Building, which opened in 1958 just after J. Lawrence Walkup became college president.

In the ensuing two decades, the college became a university and its physical plant more than doubled. This process began with the addition of new dormitories and academic buildings just south of the then existing North Campus. Other structures followed in the early 1960s, with eighteen new buildings opening in the period from 1960 to 1965. With this unprecedented growth, much of the North Campus was completed and portions of what became the Central Campus emerged. The latter included new dormitories, Central Dining, the North Activity Center (later renamed the University Union Field House), and Cline Library.

The last half of the 1960s witnessed more infilling of the Central Campus. Thirteen new structures were completed, including the NAU Bookstore, the Fronske Student Health Center, expanded facilities for the sciences, the Liberal Arts Building, and facilities for the fine and performing arts.

A second wave of expansion followed the decision to build a new campus called the South Academic Center (SAC) on land south of the existing campus. Between 1970 and 1977, twenty new structures were completed, all but three of which were part of the new campus. The SAC was self-contained with its own dormitory, dining facility, academic buildings, a small library study center, and an administrative building. The Executive Center, later named the Babbitt Administrative Center, was opened on the hill that overlooks South Campus. It is the southernmost structure of Central Campus. One of the final pieces of the building boom was the J. Lawrence Walkup Skydome, a magnificent, multipurpose facility housing athletics, performance events, local community events, and commencement ceremonies.

Following the extraordinary expansion during the Walkup era, the campus continued to grow but at a more moderate rate. From 1980 to 2009, additions included new facilities for the physical plant operations, Applied Research and Development, and the Wall Aquatic Center. A number of new residence halls for students were also added, including Mountain View Hall and Aspen Crossing. The additions from the last three decades involved filling areas of the campus. Several versions of master plans served to guide decisions about what buildings would be best located in particular spaces.

Architecture *(by Thomas Paradis)*

The variety of human environments that comprise campuses, such as that of NAU, are often defined by collections of buildings and the uses of spaces between them. Each human landscape can hold powerful meanings for the people who interact with it, and can evoke

a distinct sense of place. Grady Clay, one of America's leading scholars of American cultural landscapes, described certain types of places as *epitome districts*. In short, epitome districts are defined as places that "carry huge layers of symbols that have the capacity to pack up emotions, energy, or history into a small space" (Clay 1980, 38). As the term implies, epitome districts provide a sense of a greater place in miniature, serving as a representative of the larger whole.

One can apply the epitome district concept to NAU, an exercise that is open to multiple interpretations. Here are four candidates. Undoubtedly, there are others, of various scale and theme, depending upon one's perspective.

On a transect through the heart of campus from north to south, the four highlighted areas include (A) the *North Campus Quad*, as viewed from the north side of Old Main; (B) the *Union Plaza* area on the east side of the University Union; (C) the *University Drive Corridor*, best viewed from the front of Wilson Hall; and (D) the *South Campus Quad*, as viewed from the south (quad) side of the new W. A. Franke College of Business Administration Building. For those who enjoy access to the NAU campus, these districts are best appreciated by visiting them personally, perhaps strolling around and viewing their characteristic "emotions, energy, or history," as Grady Clay implied. Though all four epitome districts hold their association with NAU in common, each landscape provides unique experiences and lessons. For the purposes here, it is perhaps more appropriate to emphasize the architectural meanings of these places.

Epitome District A

The oldest part of campus, north of Old Main, is also the most serene. Student-centered activities have long since shifted southward, making this more of a bucolic setting for office personnel, maturing vegetation, and leisurely strolls. Looking from the area of the Old Main steps, the greensward is at the center of the campus of the 1920s, with Blome, Gammage, and opposite buildings displaying their variety of period-style revival architecture that remained popular before World War II. In 1986, this area of North Campus—focused on Old Main as the last gasp of American Victorianism—was officially listed as a historic district on the National Register of Historic Places.

Epitome District B

The next epitome district, to the south, is typically more populated and serves as NAU's "alternative transportation" corridor devoted to bike, foot, and skateboard traffic. Once an automobile intersection just north of the University Union—imagined easily by looking in the four cardinal directions—this plaza area now features a fountain, the artful Lumberjack statue moved here from the NAU Bookstore, and a new volleyball court. At center stage is the triangular modernist addition to the University Union, contributing greatly to the bustling activity here. This may be a central place, but it is also a transition zone architecturally. The campus road and trail network, to which the buildings align, takes a "dogleg" to the right here, looking north. This represents the extreme southern continuation of the original downtown street grid, aligned with the railroad tracks. Surrounding this area are a variety of postwar modernist buildings, including the Union complex, punctuated dramatically by the new Union addition. Here lies the essence of modernism and recent infill, along with ongoing attempts to improve the pedestrian and bike friendliness of the campus.

Epitome District C

A third epitome district can be interpreted along University Drive, which cuts east to west through the cluster of residential dormitories on Central Campus. The minimalist, modern-era Wilson Hall contrasts sharply with the postmodern McKay Village Apartments across the street. An infill project that replaced earlier family housing, the village's exaggerated, neo-Craftsman architecture signifies a returning interest in historicism, or the revival of past architectural styles now considered nostalgic. Unlike the seemingly randomly scattered dormitories of the 1960s and 1970s, McKay Village contains features of the new urbanism, focusing on the use of green space, pedestrian access, and visually stimulating architecture.

Epitome District D

The expansive, sunken quad of South Campus serves as a fourth epitome district, geographically separated from the rest of NAU to the north. Viewing this inviting empty open space as a significant focus, the designers of the postmodern Franke College of Business Administration Building oriented the structure to the quad rather than to McConnell Drive; a spacious patio with multiple entryways tells us that the building's south side is the "front," though the more attractive and landscaped side is seen instead from McConnell Drive. The patio has many stairs that effectively block east–west pedestrian traffic on this side of the quadrangle. Students and employees alike tend to avoid this cement monument by navigating through the grass, on their way to the food offerings at du Bois. Still, the patio provides a veritable "spillover" of student activity outside the business building and a commanding view of the original complex of Mayan-themed structures.

Though clearly ignoring the original South Campus architectural theme, the Business Administration Building and the recent Engineering Building makeover across the quadrangle indicate the evolution of postmodern architectural design. Though perhaps too expansive to offer the cozy sense of place found on North Campus, this space and the buildings that define it represent the height of postmodernism—from their rather subtle appearance by the late 1960s to the glass-dominated, sleek facades of more recent construction. One wonders about the ways in which the human landscape of South Campus will exhibit further changes in coming decades, and how such changes will necessarily reflect larger American trends and cultural values.

Changing Mission, Changing Infrastructure

A major factor influencing infrastructure additions to the campus revolves around the evolving mission of the institution. Begun as a normal school, the major needs were for dormitories for students, a classroom building, and a training school. While the mission shifted in the 1920s and 1930s, with the granting of bachelor's degrees and then master's degrees, there were only modest changes in campus infrastructure. Expansion of training in industrial arts and home management led to new buildings, and athletics facilities expanded in the 1930s and 1940s. At the time of World War II, the campus was still contained in the area we know today as North Campus, and of course, the North Union and other recent additions to that section of campus had yet to occur.

The years after the war witnessed major changes in the mission of the school. Large numbers of returning veterans were interested in diverse subjects and soon buildings appeared that functioned for specific areas within the curriculum. The education program expanded, acquiring its own building and a new training school. Sciences were housed in several structures in succession as the need for training in biology, chemistry, mathematics, geology, and physics grew. Athletics and physical education now had several structures, including a new gymnasium.

In the 1960s, the school became Northern Arizona University and, befitting the new status, considerable infrastructure changes occurred. Expansive growth of the student population at this time was a second major influence on infrastructure changes. A new library, student union, more dining facilities, and many new dormitories served the needs of students outside the classroom. Buildings for academic instruction, teaching laboratories, and research were constructed at the rate of about one per year by the end of the decade and then into the 1970s. As various academic programs evolved into separate discipline-specific departments, students completed programs of study that included majors in almost all of the subject areas that are familiar to us today, and emerging areas, such as engineering, anthropology, and nursing, formed as parts of existing departments and eventually split into their own distinct unit.

The design for a separate South Academic Center during the early 1970s brought with it the largest period of infrastructure expansion in the school's history. Some construction on the South Campus accompanied development of a separate center, some resulted from expansion of the student population, and some was brought on by changing curriculum and shifts in institutional mission.

For much of the period from the mid-1970s, when the majority of the South Campus buildings were completed, until today, the infrastructure changes involved filling in areas or replacing existing structures. The New Laboratory Facility on North Campus is an example.

Others include the construction of McKay Village Apartments and Aspen Crossing Learning Community. Other post-1975 projects, built on the edges of campus, include the Wall Aquatic Center, the Information Technology Services complex, the Applied Research and Development Building, and the multi-level parking structure. Finally, several purchases during this period added to the campus building inventory. Among these are the Ponderosa Building and Fountaine House.

The Future

As we completed this book during 2010, there were several newly completed construction projects on campus. These include an addition to the Communications Building for Distance Learning services and a complete set of recreation fields on South Campus, with lights, full drainage systems, and artificial turf.

The campus master plan provides a basis for decision making as new funds develop for infrastructure changes and additions. The vagaries of campus construction projects and the need to secure funds lead to shifts in priorities and construction plans. Recent funding from the state and ongoing bonding will support a number of projects over the next several years. These include (1) an expansion of the Recreation Center to include the Student Health Center, a Wellness Center, and several classrooms; (2) a new structure for Health Professions; (3) a series of significant renovations for the Liberal Arts Building, the Walkup Skydome, and the North Union; and (4) reconfiguring the former Inn at NAU as space for the School of Hotel and Restaurant Management. Plans are also under way for a Native American Center on campus, partially funded by several generous gifts from Arizona Native American tribes.

Unsolved Mysteries

During the research for this book, many mysteries were resolved. Some, however, were not. We would like to share these unsolved mysteries and enlist the reader's help in solving them. Here is a brief synopsis of several campus building enigmas.

Infirmaries

We know that there have been infirmaries dating back to about 1915, but the complete pattern is not certain. We know some locations, working backwards from the Fronske Student Health Center and the Moeur Infirmary, which we believe to be the structure on the north side of Dupont Street on the 1949 map. At some earlier dates, an infirmary is shown on maps among the smaller buildings located in a southward line behind Taylor Hall (see the 1949 map). Confirming these findings and filling in the locations and dates for earlier infirmaries still need completion.

Golf Course

Our research indicates that a campus golf course was under construction in the late 1930s on what was then the southeast edge of campus. The old Dairy Barn was to be the clubhouse and the milking shed would have served as the caddy shack. More information on this project would be most welcome.

W. H. Waggoner Photograph

A photograph of W. H. Waggoner would complete our set of people pictures.

As indicated in "Notes on the Organization of the Book" in the front matter, we welcome corrections and additional information on any aspect of the book.

Buildings as History:
A Note on Continuing Construction

As we approach the second decade of the twentieth century, we are in a period when construction on the NAU campus is matched only by the major developments of the Walkup era. In addition to the buildings covered in the final section of the book, there are some ongoing projects that will bring the coverage up to the end of 2010. These include (1) the Extended Campus' Facility, which is an addition to the Communications Building and was completed and opened for use in summer 2010. (2) The former Counseling and Testing Center was demolished in summer 2010. (3) That location will now be the site of a new Native American Cultural Center. This is a joint effort partnered by NAU and significant funding from Native American tribes in Arizona. (4) The Health and Learning Center, which includes an expanded Recreation Center, will be occupied in stages during the latter half of 2011 and into early 2012. This structure will house classrooms, the student health services, Employee Assistance and Wellness, Disability Resources, and includes demolition and reconstruction of the Lumberjack Stadium. (5) The North Campus Utilities Plant (known before as the Plateau Center) is undergoing extensive renovation and will include an addition to accommodate high-temperature heat and chilled air needs on North Campus. (6) A makeover of the former Inn at NAU will combine that facility into the School of Hotel and Restaurant Management for classroom and laboratory spaces. This is scheduled to be ready by spring 2011. (7) An interior renovation for the Walkup Skydome that includes a number of safety issues and replacing all of the seating is slated to begin by late December 2010 and be finished by fall 2011. (8) Finally, much of the underground infrastructure on North Campus is being updated to handle the power needs of many buildings on North Campus. This should be completed prior to the start of the 2011–2012 academic year. The North Union has undergone an infrastructure upgrade to and a significant remodel of the interior; original elements such as the masonry fireplace and original wood floors have been kept intact. The facility includes a restaurant named "The 1899," representing NAU's long history. This was completed and opened in December 2010. The Liberal Arts Building is undergoing significant improvements to the facility's learning spaces; this project will be completed in August 2011.

APPENDIX

LIST OF BUILDINGS

The appendix provides an alphabetical listing of buildings
with page references. Building numbers key to the maps;
where there is no number, the structure is not on any of
the maps.

Structure	Map Key Number	Page
Babbitt Administrative Center (Executive Center)	51	227
Bellwood Auditorium (Social and Behavioral Sciences West)	70	220
Bilby Research Center	52	240
Biological Sciences Building	21	170
Biology Annex	21B	170
Biology Greenhouse	18A	170
Blome Building (Training School, Personal Building)	2	29
Bury Hall—Residence (Offices)	8	11
Campbell Hall—Residence	6	23
Campus Heights Apartments (Dorm J)	50	139
Capital Assets and Services Building	77	248
Capital Assets and Services Annex	77A	248
Centennial Building	91	267
Ceramics Complex	80	251

Structure	Map Key Number	Page
Chemistry Building (Physical Science)	20	182
Clifford White Theatre (Performing and Fine Arts)	37	189
Cline Library	28	163
Clock (Fountain)	—	44
College of Business (Social and Behavioral Sciences West)	70	220
Communications Building (Technology and Fine Arts, Applied Science and Technology, Art and Design)	16	119
Cottage City (Stone Cottages)	108	36
Counseling and Testing Center (Psychology Annex)	26A	226
Cowden Learning Center—Residence (Dorm F, Cowden Hall)	38	144
Dairy Barn and Milking Shed	104	42
du Bois Conference Center	64	206
Eastburn Education Center	27	90

Structure	Map Key Number	Page
Education Annex	23A	94
Emerald City	98	270
Employee Assistance and Wellness (EAW) House	19A	239
Engineering and Technology Building	69	215
Eugene M. Hughes School of Hotel and Restaurant Management	33A	114
Federal Temporary Housing (Residence)	114	36
Field House	30	150
Fountaine House—Residence	89	238
Frier Hall (Science, Forestry, Geology)	12	68
Fronske Student Health Center (University Health Center)	41	159
Gabaldon Hall—Residence (the Ridge)	53	244
Gammage Building (Administration Building)	1	54
Garages	109	78

Structure	Map Key Number	Page
Gardner Auditorium	81	273
Gateway Student Success Center (University Dining, University Commons, University Avenue Dining)	43	177
Geology Annex (U.S. Forest Service Research Building)	13	72
Gillenwater Hall—Residence (South Quadrangle)	31	108
Greenhouse (original)	107	78
Greenhouse Complex	79	250
Hanley Hall (Science)	7	15
Health Professions Building (Science Building, Health Sciences)	66	196
Heating Plant (original)	101	18
Heating Plant (Plateau Center)	24	76
Heating Plant Annex and Chiller Addition	67	204
Herrington House (President's House, Counseling Center, Athletics)	102	32

NOTES ON SOURCES

In the course of locating information and photos, we consulted a variety of sources at different locations. In books of this sort, intended for a popular audience, it is customary to provide a synopsis of the sources used to gather information rather than specific citations on individual points or pages as in a more technical work. On this matter of citing sources, we used similar books done for other university campuses' guides. For this book, the following served as major sources of information (see also references at the end of the book):

From Special Collections and Archives at Cline Library, Northern Arizona University

(a) Vertical files
(b) *Arizona Champion/Coconino Sun* (Flagstaff, Arizona) newspaper obituary index (1883 to 2004) (http://www6 .nau.edu/library/da/obits/display/browseby.cfm)
(c) *La Cuesta* Yearbook (1917–1968)
(d) Annual catalogs and bulletins (1899–2008)
(e) Campus telephone directories (1968–2008)
(f) Histories of NAU—Cline, Hutchinson, Walkup (see references)
(g) Histories of Flagstaff—Cline (see references)

(h) Microfilms of the *Coconino Sun* and *Arizona Daily Sun* newspapers
(i) The Fronske Studio Photograph Collection
(j) *Lumberjack*—student newspaper (originally the *Pine*) (1913–2008)
(k) The *Pine* (as *NAU Alumni Association Magazine*) (1956–2008)
(l) Platt Cline Collection
(m) Robert Fronske Photograph Collection
(n) Arizona Historical Society photograph collection

From other sources at Northern Arizona University

Capital Assets and Services
Northern Arizona University, Department of Mathematics and Statistics, 1899–1999, by Everett L. Walter
"A Historical Account of the W. A. Franke College of Business"

From sources outside the university

Flagstaff Public Library
Library at Arizona State University
Arizona Historical Society
Theatrikos Theatre Company
World Wide Web: Internet Web sites

REFERENCES

Ashurst, H. F., and G. F. Sparks (eds.). 1962. *A Many-Colored Toga: The Diary of Henry Fountain Ashurst*. Tucson: University of Arizona Press.

Clay, G. 1980. *How to Read the American City*. Chicago: University of Chicago Press.

Cline, P. A. 1976. *They Came to the Mountain: The Story of Flagstaff's Beginnings*. Flagstaff, AZ: Northern Arizona University and Northland Press.

———. 1983. *Mountain Campus: The Story of Northern Arizona University*. Flagstaff, AZ: Northland Press.

———. 1990. *A View from Mountain Campus: Northern Arizona University in the 1980s*. Flagstaff, AZ: Northland Press.

———. 1994. *Mountain Town: Flagstaff's First Century*. Flagstaff, AZ: Northland Press.

———. 1999. *Mountain Campus Centennial*. Flagstaff, AZ: Northern Arizona University.

Hutchinson, M. T. 1972. *The Making of Northern Arizona University*. Flagstaff: Northern Arizona University.

Lewis, P. 1979. "Axioms for Reading the Landscape." In D. W. Meinig (ed.), *The Interpretation of Ordinary Landscapes*. New York: Oxford University Press, 11–32.

Lowenthal, D. 1985. *The Past Is a Foreign Country*. New York: Cambridge University Press.

Myers, J. L. (ed.) 1989. *The Arizona Governors, 1912–1990*. Phoenix: Heritage Publishers.

Paradis, T. W. 2003. *Theme Town: A Geography of Landscape and Community in Flagstaff, Arizona*. New York: iUniverse Publishing.

Smith, D. 1989. *Grady Gammage: ASU's Man of Vision*. Tempe, AZ: Arizona State University.

Tinker, G. H. 1969. *Northern Arizona and Flagstaff in 1887*. Glendale, CA: Arthur C. Clark Co.

Turner, P. 1984. *Campus: An American Planning Tradition*. Cambridge: MIT Press.

Walkup, J. L. 1984a. *Pride, Promise, and Progress: The Development of Northern Arizona University*. Flagstaff, AZ: Author Universal Publishing.

———. 1984b. "Voices of the Campus: A Supplement to the History of Northern Arizona University, 1946–1979." Flagstaff, AZ: Northern Arizona University (bound typescript).

———. 1994. *Challenges and Highlights*. Marceline, MO: Wadsworth Publishing.

Williams, T. (ed.) 1999. *Celebrating the Centennial: Centennial Yearbook*. Flagstaff, AZ: Northern Arizona University.

Lee C. Drickamer was born in Ann Arbor, Michigan, and raised in Champaign–Urbana, Illinois, as the oldest of five children in an academic family. He attended University High School and Oberlin College in Ohio, where he received his bachelor of arts degree in 1967. He obtained a doctorate from Michigan State University in zoology in 1970. His academic career includes one year of research with the North Carolina Foundation for Mental Health, fifteen years at Williams College in Massachusetts, eleven years at Southern Illinois University, and a final eleven and a half years at Northern Arizona University. He retired in December 2009. His research in the area of animal behavior included studies of primates, rodents, and birds.

Drickamer was a science administrator at Williams College, served as chair of the Department of Zoology at Southern Illinois University for four years, and was chair of the Department of Biological Sciences at Northern Arizona University for eight years. His professional service includes five years as secretary general of the International Council of Ethologists and four years in the Presidential Sequence of the Animal Behavior Society. He was recognized as the Kaplan Research Award Scholar at Southern Illinois University in 1997 and received the Exceptional Service Award from and is the 2010 recipient of the Distinguished Animal Behaviorist Award from the Animal Behavior Society.

Drickamer is the co-author of widely used textbooks in animal behavior and mammalogy. He is also co-editor of three works involving animal behavior, including a volume released in 2010 containing autobiographies of leading figures in animal behavior. His interest in history stems from a high school class and has resulted in several previous books. These include a postal history of Berkshire County in western Massachusetts and two edited books involving Civil War correspondence and commentary.

Peter Runge was born in Washington, D.C., and was raised in the Greater D.C. area and upstate New York (Schenectady). He graduated from Villanova University with bachelor's degrees in English literature and sociology. He earned a master's degree in literature from West Chester University (Pennsylvania) and a master of science in information science from the University at Albany, SUNY.

He has worked in academic and special libraries for the past ten years. He is currently the curator of manuscripts and digital content at the Cline Library, Special Collections and Archives, on the campus of Northern Arizona

University. He has been in that position since 2005. Runge has worked at several other academic special collections libraries, including the Mandeville Special Collections and Archives at the University of California, San Diego; the Special Collections and Archives department at the Schaffer Library on the campus of Union College; the M. E. Grenander Special Collections and Archives at the University at Albany, SUNY; and the library at the Knolls Atomic Power Laboratory in Niskayuna, New York.

While working in upstate New York, Runge edited and compiled, with Susan D'Entremont, the *Directory of Repositories* for the Capital District Library Council's Documentary Heritage Program. The directory is composed of institutions that provide public access to their historical records and includes listings from a wide variety of repositories in the region, including churches, colleges and universities, historical societies, libraries, museums, organizations, and others.